HISTORY OF FRECKLETON
CHURCH OF ENGLAND PRIMARY SCHOOL

HISTORY OF FRECKLETON CHURCH OF ENGLAND PRIMARY SCHOOL

Peter Shakeshaft

Dedicated to all those who have contributed to the success of the school 1839–2014

First published in 2014 on behalf of the author by
Scotforth Books (www.scotforthbooks.com)

ISBN 978-1-909817-11-1

Typesetting and design by Carnegie Book Production, Lancaster
Jacket Design by School Governors.

Printed in the UK by Short Run Press

CONTENTS

FOREWORD

FRECKLETON CHURCH OF ENGLAND PRIMARY SCHOOL is one part of the great family of schools in the Diocese of Blackburn. Along with many others, it bears testimony to the passionate concern of our forebears of the need to provide education, accessible to all, and with Christ at the centre. Today, 175 years after the foundation of the National School in Freckleton, that same passion remains as the school's reason to exist. I know from my visit, soon after taking up my post as Bishop of Blackburn, that Freckleton Church of England Primary School is committed to providing excellent education to all its pupils, with Jesus Christ at the centre of all it does.

I pray that God may bless your school in this its anniversary year and on into the future. And I pray that everyone who is part of the school community, as a pupil, parent, member of staff, governor or friend, will come to know Jesus for themselves.

+ Julian
Bishop of Blackburn

PREFACE

THIS BOOK HAS BEEN PUBLISHED to acknowledge 175 years of the school providing a formal education and schooling provision within the village of Freckleton supported by the Church of England. 175 years may appear to the reader to be an unusual period of time in which to celebrate a particular historical event, often it is usual to celebrate centennial or other centennial anniversaries. There is however a poignant significance for the decision and justification for this publication during the school's 175th anniversary year as will be outlined below.

The tragic Freckleton Air Disaster in 1944 resulted in post-disaster developments to provide on-going provision of a Church of England School in Freckleton which at that time still remained the only formal education school education in the village. Such developments included the reparation of the original school building and temporary use of other venues; the phased developments of a new school site and ultimately the closure of the original school building in 1970.

The decision and justification to publish this book on the 175th anniversary of the school permits the unique opportunity for it be accessed by three current generational groups, namely the generation who can recall the school during the periods of prior to, during and the aftermath of the disaster; the generation who can recall the transitional period involving the old school and phased development of the new school site; and the generation who will only know the school on its current site.

The book is intended to provide the most comprehensive and accurate historical account of the school based upon factual records and information available to date. Considerable research and painstaking work has been undertaken by the author which has included access to school log books and records; local and national archives; local authority and government records and papers; local and national press; evidence from individuals including documents and photographs.

As stated earlier, this publication centers on the historical provision of 175 years of formal school education in the village of Freckleton supported by the Church of England. It is important to note that although the school was the first to provide a formal provision within the village, prior to that time there were various endeavours that offered some forms of learning to individuals. In addition it is also important to note that with the growth of Freckleton the demand for formal education and schooling has led to the additions of a County Primary School and a Roman Catholic Primary School and various pre-school organisations.

This preface has been jointly compiled by the current Chair of Governors and Headteacher with the genuine intention to give recognition of the work of all their predecessors who have shaped and led in the developments of the school throughout the past 175 years. Similarly it is also a privilege to have the opportunity to give acknowledgement of the contributions given by school staff, pupils, Church, parents and all those others who have been involved with the school since 1839.

On commissioning the development of this book, Governors were clear that it was imperative that the sole aim of the book, as a school, was to add to the historical body of knowledge of Freckleton and to inform and educate others as a symbolic marker of 175 years of public service. Governors were also determined that the cost of the book should be kept to a minimum so as to make it as affordable to as many people as possible, and that sales of the book be intended to cover production and delivery costs only and not for profit-making purposes.

Special mention must be made of Frederick Arthur Billington whose headship (1939–1968) witnessed many testing times and uncertainty. He led our school through the period of World War II, the tragedy of a major disaster and unimaginable loss and the subsequent aftermath, the complex processes and work throughout the transitory phase of the formation of a new school. At all times he maintained a resolute determination of ensuring the ongoing delivery of education for the children of Freckleton during a significant period of change.

Finally, we would like to give acknowledgement to Peter Shakeshaft, as author, for giving so much of his time and energy in ensuring that this unique historical account of our school has been published.

Jim Martin — Chair of Governors
Rachael Ainsworth — Headteacher

INTRODUCTION

THIS BOOK, TO MARK THE 175TH ANNIVERSARY of the laying of the foundation stone of Trinity School, is a continuing story of dedicated service and commitment by clergy, teachers, managers, governors, and numerous other volunteers, to provide an education to the children of Freckleton. An era that now spans eight or nine generations.

A Quaker school provided a basic education for a small number of children during the mid eighteenth century. Thereafter, there was no known educational provision until the first third of the nineteenth century when a "Dames School" and a Methodist Sunday school were established.

The man charged with responsibility for the building of the first purpose built school, as he had also been for the building of Holy Trinity Church, was the Rev. George Wylie, the perpetual curate of Warton from 1830 to 1844. His endeavours were realised when the foundation stone of Trinity School was laid on 5 August 1839.

The remainder of the nineteenth century was a period of continual struggle to maintain and finance the school, as exemplified by its closure, due to lack of funding, in the early 1850s. During the late nineteenth century the headmasters Robert Lupton and James Bramwell laid the foundations of the future success of the school.

In the modern era the air disaster of 23 August 1944 is, sadly, the event for which the school is most remembered. I am aware that there were differing views, as to the future direction of education in the village, in the years immediately following the disaster. I trust therefore that the reader will recognise that I have made every effort to provide an even-handed account of the events that followed. This includes previously unpublished correspondence which records the views of those most involved in ensuring the continuation of educational provision in the village.

Nine years after the disaster the decision was made to build a new school. The foundation stone of the New Memorial School, later renamed Freckleton Church of England Primary School, was laid in 1954 and the school was subsequently built in three phases. With the opening of Phase III the original Trinity School finally closed. Two years earlier Frederick Arthur Billington had retired as headmaster after twenty nine years of dedicated service.

The twenty-first century has witnessed, and continues to witness, changes in the national educational system. These changes have placed heavy demands on teachers and governors alike. All this notwithstanding Freckleton Church of England Primary School continues to provide a fulfilling education for the children of Freckleton as it did, albeit under its original name of Trinity School, one hundred and seventy five years ago.

Documents used during the course of my research include those seen or obtained from Lancashire Archives, and National Archives, London. Local newspapers have also been a source of important information. Perhaps most valuable of all are the school log books as they provide vivid accounts of events as they were actually unfolding. For access to the log books I thank present headteacher Mrs. Rachael Ainsworth, and former headteacher Mr. Gary Worthy. Reference details for all documents quoted are listed under 'notes'.

I am particularly grateful for all those who have provided class photographs. Whilst every effort has been made to correctly name former pupils, the distance in time, from when many of the photographs were taken, inevitably means that memories have been 'stretched to the limit'. I apologise to any former pupil whose name is 'not known', but who, after this book is published, is identified. Also to anyone who has been mis-identified, or whose name has been mis-spelt. Sadly there are no class photographs from 1956 to 1983 as it would appear that commercial photographs were not taken during that period.

All other illustrations for which copyright still exists, or for which permission has been given for their use, have been duly credited.

Finally, I wish to thank Mr. Jim Martin, chair of the school governors, and Mrs. Rachael Ainsworth, the headteacher, for initiating the writing of this history, and for their support throughout the research and writing of the book.

Peter Shakeshaft

CHAPTER ONE

Education in Freckleton 1551–1839

THE FIRST RECORDED EVIDENCE of the education of children in the parish of Kirkham is in 1551 when the grammar school at Kirkham received a bequest of twenty shillings from Thomas Clifton of Westby.[1] In 1655 the school benefitted further from a bequest in the will of Henry Colborn, a scrivener in London but originally from Kirkham. Although it was the intention of Henry Colborn that his bequest be used to 'maintain schools and poor people' it is doubtful whether many boys from Freckleton, other than the sons of leading families, received an education at Kirkham until the curriculum was broadened in 1840.

In fact there is no evidence that anything was done for the poorer children of Freckleton until 1724 when the Quaker William Brown left a legacy of £300 on trust for the education of Quaker children.[2] The school was almost certainly held at the Quaker meeting house, which had been erected on the site of the present Village Memorial Hall. It is this school after which the present day School Lane is named.

The school appears to have functioned throughout the mid eighteenth century until approximately 1773 when an entry in the Quakers accounts records that 'so long as there is no Schoolmaster it's agreed that for the future one general account serve for all'.[3]

After 1773 there is no known evidence of the existence of a school at the meeting house, or elsewhere in the village, until 1803 when an entry in the sundry disbursements book for the township recorded 'To Thos Noblet giving Notice for the men to meet at School'.[4]

The purpose of this particular meeting was to decide which able-bodied men should be called upon to serve in the militia. As upwards of one hundred men would have received notice to attend, the "School" was clearly selected as the most suitable venue. It would, therefore, suggest that the building, though still owned by the Quakers, was being used either as a private school, or as a school funded by the township following cessation of regular Quaker meetings in 1796.

During the period from 1799 to 1830 Thomas Willacy, a schoolmaster, appears as executor or witness in sixteen Freckleton wills. The son of Thomas and Mary Willacy (nee Breckell) he was born in Freckleton in 1764, and although he served continuously as either the township constable or overseer of the poor from 1794 to 1827 nothing is known of his early life. He does not appear to have married, and probably lived with his two unmarried sisters in a cottage which stood on the site of the present day (2014) Methodist Church.

In the Lancashire Directory of 1828 Thomas Willacy was recorded as a 'schoolmaster, Freckleton – boy's day'. The assumption that this school was being held in the Quaker meeting house is supported by the entry in the 1829 Survey of Dissent which reported that the meeting house was indeed then being used as a school.[5] Whether Thomas Willacy leased this building on his own account, or whether the township paid him to operate the school is again unknown.

When he died in 1831 his will was proved by George Richardson, one of the leading Methodists in Freckleton at that time. There is, however, no evidence to suggest that Thomas Willacy was himself a member of the local Methodist community.

Following his death it would appear that the members of the Wesleyan Methodist congregation (the first Methodist chapel had opened in 1814) endeavoured to take over the role of providing education for the village children. The Methodist Sunday school class registers for 1833 lists the names of 69 boys and 68 girls who, in addition to Bible and Testament classes also attended Double-spelling book Class; Single-spelling book Class; and Alphabet Class. In all there were nineteen classes taught by adult members of the Methodist community.[6]

By this date it had become apparent to the Very Rev. Dr James Webber, (vicar of Kirkham 1813–1847) that there was a pressing need for a permanent presence of the Church of England in Freckleton. As early as 1828 he had advised Christ Church, Oxford, the patrons of Kirkham Church, that 'A dissenting place of Worship has been erected in Freckleton within a few years and it is much to be feared that the Inhabitants who are much on the increase will either be estranged from the Establishment or perhaps become indisposed to Religion altogether'.[7]

Two years later (1830) vicar Webber appointed the Rev. George Wylie as perpetual curate of Warton, with additional responsibility for Freckleton. Shortly after his appointment Rev. Wylie appears to have begun classes in the Quaker meeting house. Evidence that such classes were indeed being held is supported by the statement, recorded some years later, that 'This[meeting house] was used for some time [by the Quakers], and then the Church of England and Wesleyans used it as a [Sunday] school, each body having one end [of the building].[8]

CHAPTER TWO

The early years of Trinity School

DURING THE FIRST THIRD of the nineteenth century the population of Freckleton increased from 561 in 1801 to 909 in 1831. It continued to grow rapidly during the 1830s reaching 995 by 1841, when there were 108 children, approximately eleven per cent of the population, between the ages of five and nine years. Assuming a similar population breakdown in 1831, there would be some one hundred children of similar age in Freckleton for whom there were no daily educational facilities.

The Rev. George Wylie, who throughout the fourteen years of his curacy (1830–1844), committed himself to the people of Freckleton, thus inherited a situation where, unlike all neighbouring townships – Kirkham, Bryning with Warton, Ribby with Wrea, and Newton with Scales – there was neither church nor church school. His first challenge was to raise monies for the building of a church, which he achieved in 1837 when the foundation stone was laid of the present Holy Trinity Church.

It would seem that simultaneously with raising funds for the building of Holy Trinity Church the Rev. Wylie was also active in raising funds for the building of a church school. On 23 January 1838 he sent an 'Application for Assistance' to the 'Right Honourable the Lords of Her Majesty's Treasury' seeking additional monies in order to proceed.[9]

In his request Rev. Wylie pointed out 'that this District is likely to become more populous on account of the erection of a Manufactury in the Township [of Freckleton]', but 'that there was no provision existing for the education of the poor in which instruction may be given gratuitously on Sundays, and during the week on such low terms as may render it available to all'.

He added 'that there being no charitable endowments, public or private,

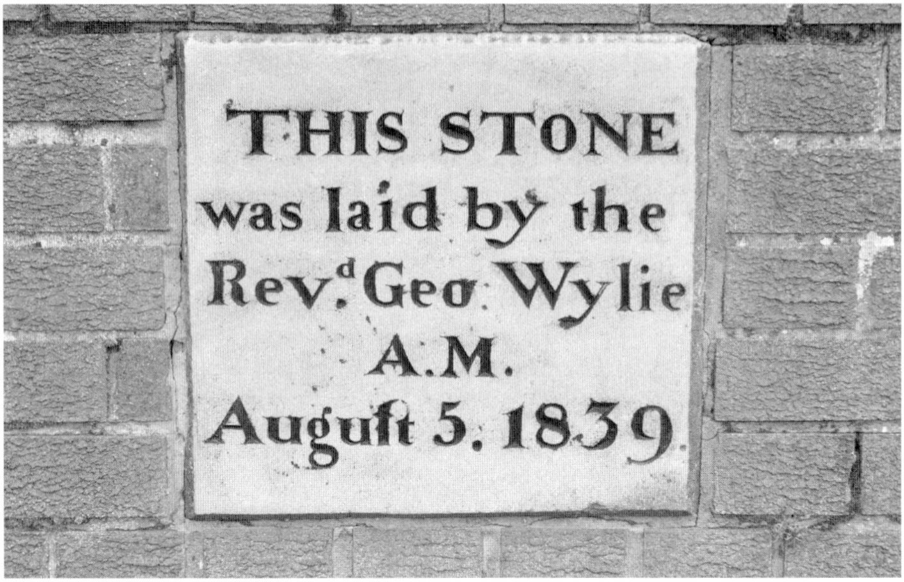

Foundation Stone – Trinity School
The foundation stone for the original Trinity School was laid on 5 August 1839 by the Rev. George Wylie, perpetual curate of Warton. It was Rev. Wylie who was tasked with the responsibility for the building of the school. The stone is now set into Holy Trinity churchyard wall.
Photograph by Brian Hudson.

in the said Township for the purposes of education, and the population (consisting principally of weavers, spinners, sailors and a few small farmers) exceedingly poor', he was 'compelled to seek from other sources the funds for the erection of such school', and that he had 'in consequence made application for a grant' to 'The Incorporated Society for the education of the poor in the principles of the Established Church'.

Rev. Wylie concluded his submission by trusting that the Lords of Her Majesty's Treasury 'may deem' his request 'not unworthy of their consideration, and afford such aid as may enable him to accomplish an undertaking at once in accordance with the object of their annual [Government] Grant, and certain to promote most materially the welfare of the District of which he is Incumbent'.

An extract of the correspondence between Rev. Wylie and the Incorporated Society (usually known as the National Society) was associated with the application to the Treasury. The extract noted that there was no provision for the education of children 'except by Dames school, and a Methodist Sunday School'.

It was proposed that a school, rectangular in shape, be built of 'Brick, Flags,

Slates', and 'receive at least 63 boys and 63 girls in two rooms'.[10] The "two rooms" were possibly one large school-room divided by a partition, each "room" measuring nineteen feet long, twenty feet wide, and thirteen feet high.

It was further proposed that the building be used as a 'Sunday school and a Daily school', and that the property be 'duly' secured 'for the education of the poorer classes under Trustees'. The annual expenses of the school were to be defrayed by 'annual subscription, and the payments from the Parents of the children [by means of school pence]'.[11]

The estimated cost of the undertaking, and which probably included the schoolmaster's house, was £290. But it was pointed out that the means to meet the cost, 'after every exertion has been made' did not amount to more than £160, leaving a deficiency of £130.[12] It may be that the dimensions of the classrooms were made slightly larger than as stated in the submission to the Treasury, and this probably accounts for the fact that some years later it was noted that the cost of the building had been £350.[13]

Presumably further fund-raising took place during the period from February 1838 to August 1839, including a grant of £40 from the National Society. And on 5 August 1839 (almost certainly Club Day) the school foundation stone, now set into Holy Trinity churchyard wall, was laid by the Rev. Wylie. The datestone, which now stands by the entrance to the present school, reads '1839 Trinity School' (the name by which it was originally known).

The school was indeed founded under the principles of the National Society which was itself founded in 1811 with, as we have seen, the stated aim of 'educating the children of the poor in the principles of the Established Church'. In 1828 the Society issued a statement which noted that 'The object in forming Establishments of this nature which now happily exists in almost every Parish and District throughout the Kingdom is

1. To train the infant Poor to good and orderly habits;
2. To instill into their minds an early knowledge of their civil and religious duties;
3. To guard them from seduction and vice; and
4. To afford them the means of becoming good Christians.'

By 1851 the National Society controlled over 17,000 national schools.

The contractor for the school was Thomas Catterall, who was also contractor for Holy Trinity Church. In a letter, dated 10 August 1839, to James Fair, the agent to the Clifton family of Lytham Hall, concerning alterations to Warton Church, Rev. Wylie wrote 'Shall I be asking too much if I beg the same favour in the case of my new school at Freckleton for which Catterall is also a contractor? As far as he is concerned there will be no gain – he gives the value of the sand [carted from Lytham] to the school'.[14]

The land on which the school was built, part of a close called the Higher Croft, now (2014) the site of Trinity Close, was conveyed by the legal procedure of lease and release. The lease was completed on 1 January 1840 when Joseph Hornby and Hugh Hornby Birley granted a lease of the land, for one year, to Joseph Briggs Dickson, a Preston attorney, acting on behalf of Hugh Hornby. This indenture is particularly interesting as it provides evidence, by referring to 'a School or Edifice called Trinity School lately erected', that the school was then already built.[15]

On 2 January 1840 Joseph Hornby and Hugh Hornby Birley completed the release to Hugh Hornby. On 4 November 1840 Hugh Hornby, and his trustee, leased the same to the Rev. Wylie and others. Any significance of this latter date, in the absence of more detailed documentation, is unknown.

Although, as we have seen, Trinity School (also known as the National School) had been erected by late 1839 no master, or mistress, had been appointed. And it was not until March 1840 that the following notice appeared in the *Preston Pilot*

> Wanted, A Master and Mistress for the New National School at Freckleton, in the parish of Kirkham. A Master whose wife could undertake the charge of the Girls' School would have the preference.
>
> Salary for the two, £40, with a small house.
>
> Applications, with testimonials, to be forwarded immediately to the Rev. George Wylie MA, Incumbent of Warton, addressed to the care of the Rev. J. R. Echlin, Freckleton.[16]

The school trustees subsequently appointed John Worthington, who was born at Medlar with Wesham in 1816, and Elizabeth Green, who was born at Carleton in 1815, as master and mistress of Trinity School. When they were married at All Hallows, Bispham, on 13 June 1840, their occupations were recorded as 'Master of the National School, Freckleton', and 'Schoolmistress of the same place'.[17]

The actual date of when the school opened has not been ascertained, but, on the evidence of a notice in the *Preston Pilot*, it was probably between 16 April 1840 (Easter Sunday), and 30 May 1840

> On Sunday 7th June 1840 Two Sermons will be preached at Trinity Church, Freckleton by the Rev. Prince Crawford M.A., Incumbent of St Saviour's, Liverpool
>
> In aid of the Funds for completing the National School lately opened in that Township, when the attendance of all Friends of sound and Scriptural Education is earnestly required.

Divine Service will commence at half-past ten o'clock in the Morning, in the Afternoon at half-past two.[18]

Following their marriage John and Elizabeth Worthington occupied the previously mentioned 'small house' adjacent to the school. In 1843 the Rev. Wylie supported the candidature of John Worthington as assistant overseer at Poulton.[19] However, John Worthington was still master in 1845, and it may have been that, in order to supplement his income, he combined the role of master with that of assistant overseer.

The initial enthusiasm with which the opening of the school was met can be seen in a letter written by the Rev. Thomas Henry Dundas (then perpetual curate, but subsequently first vicar of the united parish of Warton with Freckleton). Dated 24 July 1845, the letter unfortunately does not name the intended recipient, but it was almost certainly the previously mentioned James Fair. The person named Green [sic] in the letter was probably Thomas Greene, the chapelwarden at Holy Trinity. The letter reads[20]

My Dear Sir

I would thank you to send me if convenient the subscription which Green kindly promised on the part of Mr Clifton to Freckleton School & pray return him My sincere thanks for his assistance.

You will be glad to hear that the school is getting on almost as well as I could wish it numbers at present between boys and girls within two or three of a hundred. The Vicar of Preston visited it a few days since & almost promised me assistance from The Diocesan board of education in the Sum of £10 yearly, which is their largest grant, this will almost though not quite cover expenses the salaries of Master & Mistress above what the School pays, amounting to £5 above that sum.

I have however the best hopes of its final Success – with many thanks for your aid

Believe Me

Truly Yours

T .H. Dundas

As has already been mentioned, the number of children in the village in 1841, aged between five and nine years, was one hundred and eight. Assuming a similar age range and numbers in 1845, then Trinity School had achieved a significant attendance within a few years. Not even the required weekly payment seems to have deterred parents from parting with the few valuable pence necessary to enable each child to attend.

In June 1847 Rev. Dundas wrote to Christ Church, Oxford (the patrons of Warton Church) and advised them that in two years he had raised the annual subscription (donations) for the school from £4 or £5 to £30, and consequently had been able to pay a master £40 and a mistress £26 a year. He added that the average attendance of boys and girls was eighty four, but that the weekly pence had been low owing 'to the poverty of the place'. He requested the Dean & Chapter of Christ Church to replace the grant of £10 by Chester Diocesan Education Board which had been discontinued.[21]

The names of the masters and mistresses who followed John and Elizabeth Worthington are known only from entries in various trade directories. Thomas Walmsley was master from 1848 until at least 1851, and Isabella Anderton was mistress in 1848. They appear to have been followed in 1851 by James Bryan and Ann Lewis.

School outings on the Tuesday following Club Day would seem to have been a feature of the school year. Adam Wright, who had been born in Freckleton in 1796, and who wrote regularly to his nephew and nieces from Constantinople where he was a merchant banker, refers to such an event in a letter dated 3 August 1848, 'and I understand the Freckleton children join a train [at Kirkham] that day and go to Blackpool, Agnes Goodshaw [the school mistress] goes with them.[22]

Four years later, on 28 October 1852, ownership of the land on which the school stood was transferred, presumably by Hugh Hornby, to Thomas Dyson Hornby and Hugh Frederick Hornby.[23] It is unclear whether this event was directly or indirectly responsible, but shortly afterwards the steady progress which the school appeared to have been making came to an abrupt halt due to a lack of funding.

During at least part of the time during which Trinity School was closed an academy was opened and run by James Threlfall. The Freckleton township survey of 1853 indicates that this was held in a cottage located approximately on the present day (2014) open space adjacent to the gable end of Lorenzo's restaurant at the junction of Kirkham Road and School Lane.

James Threlfall was born at Freckleton in 1830, the son of William and Jane Threlfall. How he came to open and finance an academy is not known. Evidence that he did so is provided by the *Preston Chronicle* which on 13 August 1853 reported that

> Monday last, being Freckleton club day, Mr Threlfall, of Freckleton, entertained the pupils of his academy with buns and coffee; and promised to give them a trip on the following day … . Early

JAMES THRELFALL
James Threlfall was born at Freckleton in 1830. From c1853 to c1856, when Trinity School was closed due to lack of funding, he opened an academy in the village. He also paid for children's Club Day treats in 1853 and 1854. He later became headmaster of Esprick Church of England School. It is intriguing, in view of his commitment to the children of Freckleton, as to the reason why he was not appointed headmaster of Trinity School when it re-opened in 1856.

Courtesy of Mrs. Edith Wood of Great Eccleston, great granddaughter of James Threlfall. Per Mrs. Barbara Moor.

> therefore, on Tuesday morning, the pupils, accompanied by many of their parents and friends, to the number of about 250 proceeded to Lytham in fifteen conveyances of different kinds. On reaching Mrs Hornby's, the Ship Inn [Lytham], the whole party were regaled with an ample supply of bun, coffee, and other etceteras, after which they separated in groups to amuse themselves as their various fancies suggested ... . The party enjoyed themselves until six o'clock, when ... they wended their way back to their own little village. Arrived there, the whole cavalcade drew up on the spacious green, where some hundreds of the villagers, of all ages, had assembled to welcome them. The evening hymn was there sung; and three hearty cheers being given for the respected tutor, the party separated ... .[24]

A similar event took place the following year, including the singing of the evening hymn on the village green. On this occasion the *Preston Chronicle* noted that the event 'reflects credit alike on the feelings that subsist between

Mr. Threlfall and the parents of the children committed to his care, and will doubtless, tend to strengthen the bond of unity between them'.[25]

A contributory factor, with regard to the difficulties in providing sufficient funds for a master and / or mistress at Trinity School, had been the onset of ill-health of the Rev. Dundas. And in 1853 he appointed the Rev. Richard Hodgson as his curate in charge at both Warton and Freckleton.

Although, in January 1854, the Rev. W. L. Hussey (vicar of Kirkham) had had to advise Christ Church, Oxford that 'The church school has been shut up for want of funds to provide a master',[26] it is clear that between 1854 and 1856 considerable efforts were made to re-open the school, and in December 1856 the following letter, entitled 'Freckleton School', appeared in the *Preston Chronicle*

> Sir, – As the above school has recently undergone extensive alterations, at the expense of the kind and benevolent incumbent [the Rev. Richard Hodgson], whose actions of generosity are unbounded, permit me, through the medium of your journal, to say a word or two to the Frecklétonians to induce them to make an additional improvement, as an acknowledgement for the many favours conferred on them by their generous pastor.
>
> It will be admitted by all acquainted with the school that it is very damp and unhealthy, particularly at this season of the year, owing principally to the manner in which it is heated. The fires, being only a few feet apart, do little or no good; instead of being a comfort, as such ought to be in a school, they are often a nuisance. Think, for a moment, on the condition of a hundred children confined to a room where sometimes you cannot see from one end to the other, for smoke. The consequence is, that the parents are careless about sending their children, and well they may; but then, such an obstruction ought not to exist, and a sure way to remove it would be to place a stove in either division, similar to the one in the church.
>
> Let a subscription be raised amongst the inhabitants; I am sure that such a praiseworthy object would meet with their support. Let the churchwardens or the schoolmaster be appointed to collect the same, with as little delay as possible, in order that the school may be made comfortable for the reception of the rising generation after the Christmas holidays; and then the parents plea for the anomalous attendance of their children will rest with themselves, and not the school.[27]

The letter was signed by 'A Working Man', and dated Esprick, Dec. 16, 1856.

The following week, 'An Observer', from Kirkham, suggested that it might have been more appropriate for the letter to have been addressed privately 'to the authorities, instead of through the press'.[28] This in turn was replied to by 'A Working Man' who, apart from chiding 'An Observer' with not being 'conversant with the good people of Freckleton', explained that 'such address has been made, not only by myself, but by many of the Freckletonians also; and such not producing any beneficial result, I was induced, through their supplication, during a recent visit, to have recourse to the public press'.[29]

The clue to the identity of 'A Working Man' lies in the fact that he resided at Esprick. He was almost certainly the previously mentioned James Threlfall. When he married Alice Houghton at St Paul's, Warton in 1857 James Threlfall's place of residence was amended, in the register, from Freckleton to Esprick. His occupation was recorded as 'schoolmaster', presumably at Esprick National (Church of England) School. It is intriguing as to the reason why he was not appointed schoolmaster at Trinity School when it re-opened in 1856. Perhaps he had upset too many people in his public demonstrations of support for the school.

It is however the Rev. Richard Hodgson who deserves the credit for his commitment in enabling Trinity School to be re-opened. At a farewell presentation in 1858, on the occasion of his leaving Warton and Freckleton, it was recorded that 'The schools [at Warton and Freckleton] have greatly increased in numbers and usefulness; a large free library has been established; night schools for adults have been taught during the winter months; and many other useful and praiseworthy efforts for good have been made, and have been very successful'.[30]

Thomas Cumberland, who had been appointed schoolmaster at the re-opening of the school, invited the assembled audience to compare Trinity School 'now with what it was three years ago. Look at it inside and out. The master's house, the walled inclosure, the draining, and its transformation from a mere wilderness to what a school ought to be, all his [Rev. Hodgson's] work.[31]

The Rev. Hodgson was followed as curate in charge, at Warton and Freckleton, by the Rev. John Henry Ransome. But when he too resigned, Rev. Dundas, who had been absent for many years due to his continuing ill health and was then residing at Lytham, again became responsible for Trinity School. In March 1861 he sent a statement of the expenditure and receipts of the school for the year 1860 to Christ Church, Oxford, adding that he hoped that they would see fit 'with their usual kindness' to 'renew their liberal donation of £10.[32]

The 1860 accounts, as prepared by Rev. Dundas, provide a rare insight into the straitened financial circumstances at that time.

Receipts		Expenditure	
Subscriptions & Donations	£ s d		£ s d
Colonel Clifton	5 0 0	Repairs & School Expenses	3 15 2½
Dean & Chapter of Christ Church	10 0 0	Stores & fittings	2 8 9
Rev. W.L.Hussey	2 2 0	Proportion of £10 from April to December to two young teachers	7 10 0
Miss. Marquis	1 1 0	Masters Salary	48 0 0
Mr. Wright	1 1 0	Mistress for half days	17 15 0
Mr. Shaw	1 1 0	Complete set of Books Maps etc etc	12 19 10
			--------
			92 8 9½
Mr. Meyors (Mr. Mayor)	1 1 0		
Collections in Church	2 2 0		68 13 11
	-------		--------
	23 4 0		23 14 10½
School fees Boys	20 7 1		
Ditto Girls	18 8 10		
Return from Books & other Casual	5 6 0		
	-------		
	67 3 11		
Pew Rents H Hornby Esq an endowment	1 10 0		
	-------		
	68 13 11		

The schoolmaster then was Wilfred Lees, who had been appointed to the post in 1859. When he resigned in April 1861 it was said that he had 'efficiently and successfully discharged the functions of his office, being a most skilful and energetic teacher'.[33] In the same year (1861) the Rev. Walter Scott was appointed by Rev. Dundas to be the curate at Holy Trinity. Rev. Scott's appointment meant that for the first time there was a clergyman, resident in the village, with responsibility for Trinity School.

It is unclear who succeeded Wilfred Lees. On the 1861 Freckleton census Thomas Parkinson, born in Freckleton in 1838, is described as a certificated schoolmaster living with his father in Higher (Kirkham) Road. However, whilst he might have held a temporary post at Trinity School there is no evidence that it was a permanent appointment.

In 1861 school attendance was not compulsory, but in the following year the government introduced the Revised Code in an attempt to encourage attendance. Under this code payments, known as "payments by results", were made to schools based on the attendance of pupils, and on the outcome of annual examinations of the pupils. Due to an absence of any school records for the early 1860s, it is not known when the code was introduced at Trinity School.

The next master who can definitely be associated with the school was Charles Everson. One of the first demands placed on him was to assist in mitigating the distress of the operatives, employed at the village cotton factory, during the Lancashire Cotton Famine. From November 1862 to January 1864 he was secretary of the Freckleton Relief Committee.[34]

At Christmas 1862 the committee had on their books upwards of two hundred persons (the population of Freckleton in 1861 was 879), whom they relieved at the rate of 9½d. (4p.) per week. Relief was distributed to a maximum of two hundred and ninety four "cases" on 7 January 1863, and continued until December 1863.[35]

It must have been a particularly difficult time for Charles Everson as he witnessed the deprivations inflicted on the children of Trinity School. By early 1864 the distress had abated and Charles Everson appears to have resigned as master shortly afterwards. The two other members of staff also resigned at about the same time. In October 1863 the *Preston Chronicle* reported that Rebecca Cookson, the daughter of William Cookson of Further Ends Farm, had been presented 'with two handsome volumes of books by the members of her class, as a token of their appreciation of her valuable services and excellent character'.[36]

Agnes Goodshaw, who, as schoolmistress, had had an important role, particularly in the education of the girls, also retired. As we have seen she had been mistress from at least 1848. Born in Freckleton in 1820 she was the grand-daughter of James Goodshaw, co-partner of the local company Goodshaw & Mayor. On 2 January 1864 the *Preston Pilot* reported that the teachers and scholars of 'Freckleton Parish Church School' held their annual tea party in the school room, when '100 sat down'. After 'the repast' Miss Goodshaw was presented 'with a beautiful electro-plated copper pot and card case'.[37]

Charles Everson was succeeded as master by John Heron. Agnes Hall, the sister of John Hall, the owner of Strike Farm, was mistress in 1864 and 1865.

This lack on continuity of both masters and mistresses was typical of the time, and cannot have been to the advantage of the scholars. Some children did not attend school at all, as typified by George Wylie Rigby, born at Freckleton in 1858, and who in 1941 was reported as saying that 'Beginning to earn his living at the age of twelve, he never attended a day school, his only lessons being learned from the local schoolmaster on certain nights a week'.[38]

By the mid 1860s it was obvious that the school was in urgent need of an extension combined with renovation of the existing exterior, a view previously expressed by the Rev. V. Hadley, a former inspector of the school, who had considered the building 'not to be sufficiently large for the accommodation of the children'.[39] Another problem at this time was that Freckleton was still a chapelry in the parish of Warton. Consequently, it was the vicar of Warton, and his churchwardens, who continued to be the trustees of Trinity School.

This unsatisfactory arrangement was partially resolved when, on 3 May 1867, the land on which the school stood was conveyed by Thomas Dyson Hornby and Hugh Frederick Hornby to the vicar of Warton and his churchwardens, and vested in The Official Trustee of Charity Lands who directed that the school be used

> solely as and for a school for the instruction, subject to and in accordance with the provisions of this Scheme, of children and adults, or children only, of the labouring, manufacturing, and other poorer classes in the above-mentioned Ecclesiastical Districts of Freckleton and Warton respectively, a preference being at all times given to persons being inhabitants of the aforesaid Ecclesiastical District or Parish of Freckleton[40]

As a result of this ruling by The Official Trustee a Freckleton Committee of Management (the school managers) was appointed to oversee the daily running of the school. The committee comprised the Rev. Scott as school correspondent; the chapelwardens Edward Ward and Robert Moon (of Poulton); and William Cookson and Threlfall Mayor, who, as trustees, were required every year to contribute at least twenty shillings to the funds of the school. In addition the committee was permitted to select an additional committee of 'ladies' to assist them in the management of the girls and infants.

Immediately following its formation the school management committee agreed to enlarge the school with the addition of an extra classroom, and also to replace the flag floor with boarding. One hundred and forty ratepayers out of total number of two hundred and sixty six subscribed to the school extension.

Plans prepared at the time (1867) show that, prior to the extension, the school comprised a girls school-room, on the east side of the building, which measured twenty five feet by thirty feet, and a boys school-room, on the west side, which measured twenty five feet by twenty feet. The school-rooms were probably still divided by a partition, and boys and girls each had a separate entrance. A smaller room jutting out from the main building on the north side,

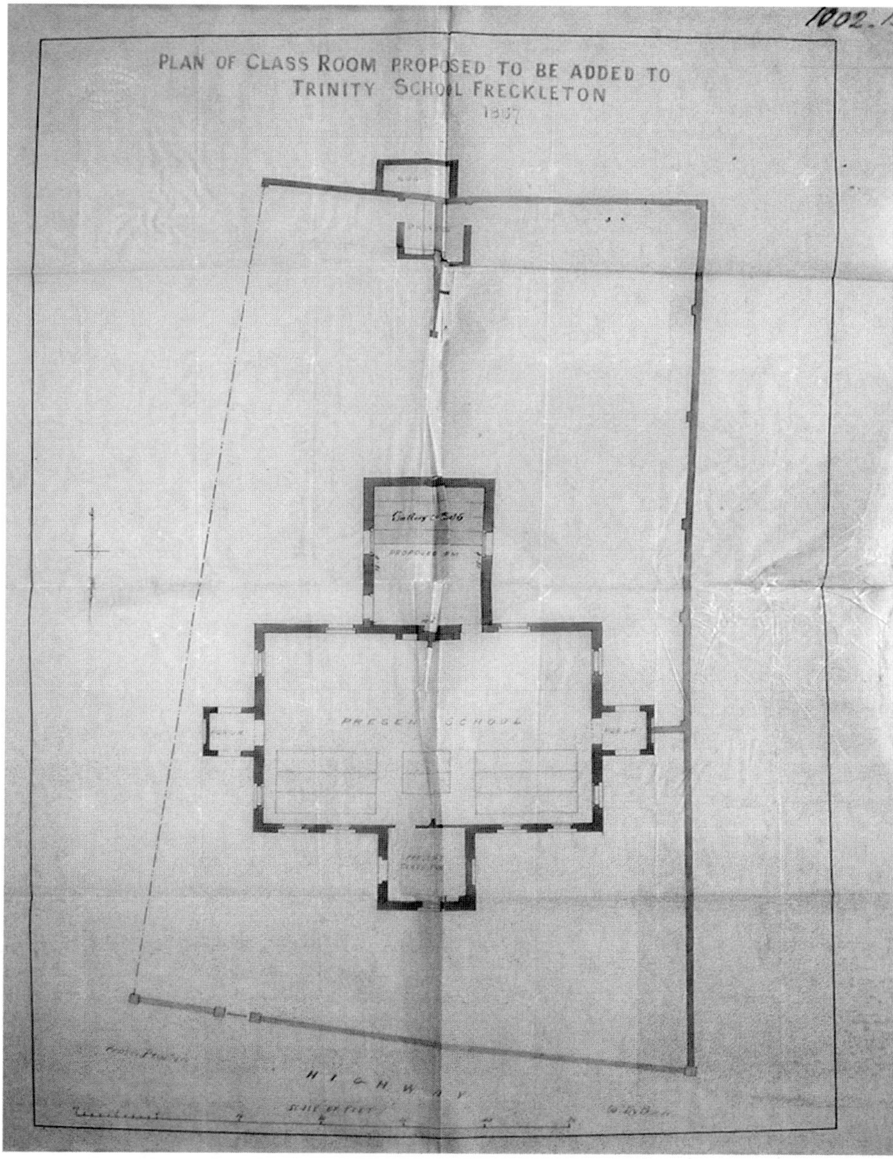

SCHOOL PLANS 1867

Plans prepared in 1867 show that, prior to the extensions, the school comprised a girls school-room and a boys school-room. Boys and girls each had their own entrance. The earth privies (toilets) were located along the south wall of the schoolyard. In 1867 new additions included a gallery. The work cost £116 10s. 0d. (£116-50p)

Courtesy of Archives Service Manager, Lancashire Archives – ref SP120.

measuring eleven feet by nine feet six inches, had also been added by this date. The earth privies were located alongside the south wall of the school yard.[41]

By September 1867 the managers had raised £61 16s. 8½d. comprising £26 3s. 7d. from voluntary local subscriptions; £2 11s. 4½d. from collections in church; £2 12s. 3d. in receipts from a concert; and £30 9s. 6d. from contributions outside Freckleton. This combined amount of £61 16s. 8½d. left a deficiency of £48 18s. 3½d. of the £110 15s.0d. estimated to carry out the work.[42]

On 12 September 1867 the Rev. Scott wrote to The Lords of the Committee of Council on Education requesting financial assistance towards meeting the deficiency. In his submission he advised the Council on Education that the aim was to increase the accommodation in order to accommodate forty boys, thirty seven girls, and thirty two infants.

Rev. Scott further advised the Council on Education that his parishioners, 'the labouring portion of which are chiefly employed as sailors, rope-makers, carpenters, shoe-makers, tailors, and labourers', did not have the means to provide any further financial assistance.

He added that the school staff comprised 'one Master, one Mistress, three Monitors', and that his committee were 'in correspondence with a young person 14 years of age who if he suit will be a Candidate next year for a Pupil Teachership'.[43]

With regard to the future support of the school Rev. Scott anticipated that 'after a careful estimate', his management committee expected to obtain 'at least the following Sums' annually

From annual Subscriptions and Donations	£7
From annual Collections	£7
From School-pence	£40
Total	£54

Having considered the request from the management committee the Council of Education gave a grant of £40 2s. 9d., which, together with the monies already in hand, and with an additional £9 5s. 2d. from the sale of the flags from the original classroom floor, enabled work to commence. And by early 1868 an additional classroom with gallery had been added on to the south side of the school.

The addition of a gallery – presumably a stepped arrangement – would have allowed full view of the pupils, and which, if the desks had been set in blocks, have permitted two or more classes to be taught simultaneously. The architects were Myres Veevers Myres of Preston whose fee was £5 15s. 0d. The total cost was £116 10s. 0d., an increase of only £4 15s 0d. on the original estimate.[44]

Trinity School re-opened on 1 April 1868 under the headship of Robert

Lupton who had been appointed master in about 1865. Born at Burnley he was aged twenty three when he came to Freckleton. His sister Hannah acted as school mistress. The number of children attending the school was recorded as 'under the Master forty boys, under the Mistress of the Girls' Department thirty eight girls, and under the Mistress of the Infants Department forty two'.[45]

It is regrettable that not more is known of Robert Lupton's time at Freckleton. That he was held in the highest regard is amply revealed in the following extracts of the newspaper report of his death, from scarlet fever, in October 1874

> When his death was announced to the children in school every child was in tears, and their sobs were most pitiful; so greatly was he loved by them.
>
> Since his coming to Freckleton, Mr. Lupton has succeeded in improving both the tone and numbers of the school. His zeal and energy were untiring.
>
> In all works of charity, in collecting for widows and orphans – of which there are several in the place – he was the first and foremost.
>
> He has been instrumental in having a new floor, new classrooms, and new desks for his school. The master's residence has been by him greatly improved.[46]

CHAPTER THREE

Victorian reform and compulsory education

THE NINE YEARS WHICH SPANNED Robert Lupton's time as master of Trinity School were also watershed years in education in England and Wales. The Elementary Education Act of 1870 set the framework for the schooling of all children between the ages of five and twelve. There were required standards of education that ranged from Standard I to Standard VI. The Act was also responsible for placing a requirement on schools to record details of school life in a school log book.

The revolutionary provision of the Act was the setting up of secular school boards which were popularly elected. School boards were also able to build their own schools. In addition many larger boroughs imposed bye-laws making education compulsory, that in turn increased revenue, since grants were related to attendance. There were, however, various objections to universal education. Board schools were subject to a clause 'No religious catechism or formulary which is distinctive of any particular denomination should be taught in the school'.

Because of this clause the Church of England, which was funded by the state with public money to provide education for the poor, and did not want to lose its influence on young people, was determined to keep the school boards at bay. Their concerns were partially addressed when, following a change of government in 1874, the Elementary Education Act of 1876 was passed which assisted voluntary rural schools, such as Trinity School, by placing the responsibility of attendance on parents.

The Act of 1876, however, insisted on the establishment of School Attendance Committees (though, as we shall see, this was not implemented at Freckleton

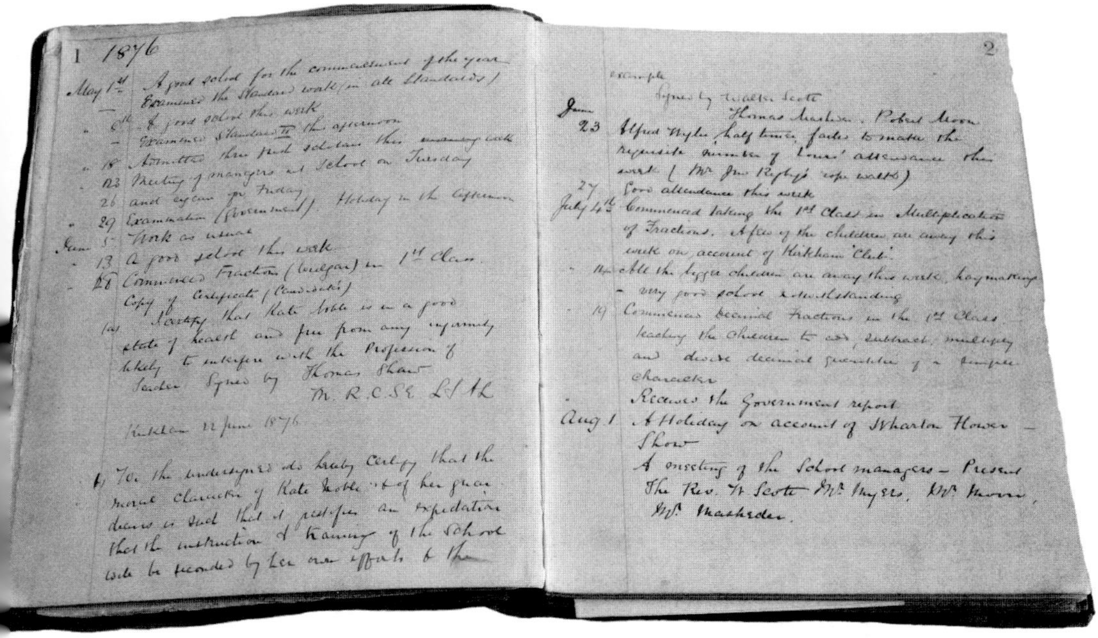

Opening page of earliest school log book – 1876

School log books, the purpose of which was to record day to day events at the school, had been in use since the 1860s, but do not appear to have been kept at Trinity School until 1876. In this latter year school inspections became the responsibility of government inspectors who put greater emphasis on the keeping of log books. The first entry for Trinity School is on 1 May 1876 when Mr. Martin, the headmaster, noted that it was 'a good school [attendance] for the commencement of the [school] year'.

School Archives. Photograph by Mrs. Nicole Partridge BA(Hons) of N. Spire Design Ltd.

until 1878) where school boards had not been established. And it required parents to ensure their children received efficient instruction.

Penalties were imposed upon parents whose children of ten years of age and up to thirteen years of age did not hold a certificate of proficiency in the "three R's" (Reading, wRiting, aRithmetic), or a certificate of due attendance at a certified efficient school. The Act also resulted in regular Government inspection.

In 1876 William Moorhouse Martin, who had succeeded Robert Lupton in 1874, was master at Trinity School. He lived at the school house with his sister Emily, who was the school mistress. It was Mr. Martin who commenced the school log book in 1876, thereby providing, for the first time, a detailed account of day to day life at the school.[47]

One of the earliest entries in the log book is a transcription of the report

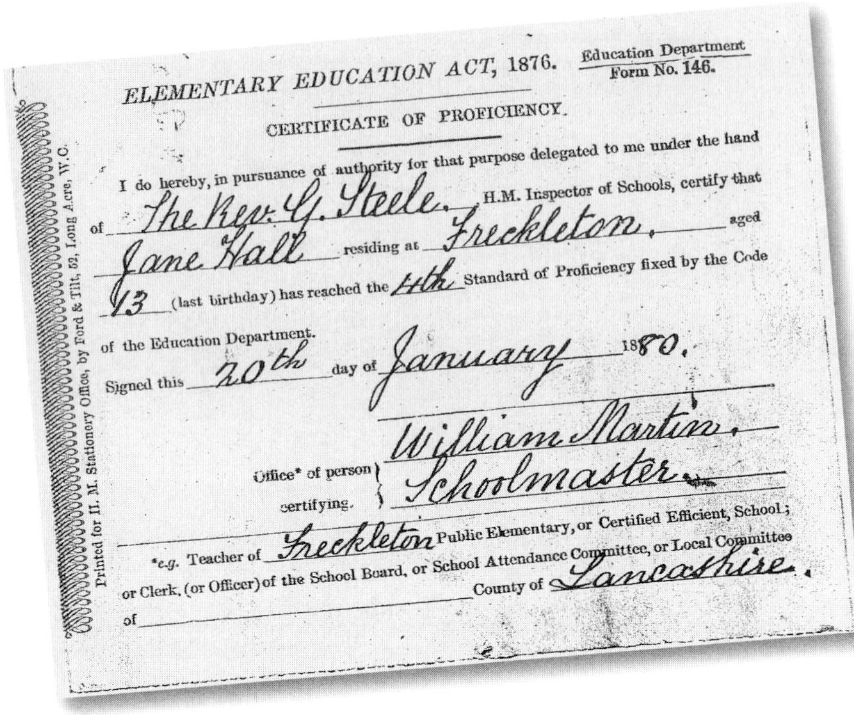

ELEMENTARY EDUCATION ACT, 1876. Education Department Form No. 146.

CERTIFICATE OF PROFICIENCY.

I do hereby, in pursuance of authority for that purpose delegated to me under the hand of The Rev. G. Steele. H.M. Inspector of Schools, certify that Jane Hall residing at Freckleton. aged 13 (last birthday) has reached the 4th Standard of Proficiency fixed by the Code of the Education Department.

Signed this 20th day of January 1880.

William Martin.

Office* of person certifying. Schoolmaster.

*e.g. Teacher of Freckleton Public Elementary, or Certified Efficient, School; or Clerk, (or Officer) of the School Board, or School Attendance Committee, or Local Committee of ________ County of Lancashire.

Printed for H. M. Stationery Office, by Ford & Tilt, 52, Long Acre, W.C.

Proficiency certificate of Jane Hall

The Education Act of 1880 made school attendance compulsory for all children up to the age of ten years. At the age of ten a child could obtain a certificate of proficiency and become a "half-timer". At the age of thirteen years they were eligible for full time employment. For most girls in Freckleton during the period 1880 to 1920 this meant employment at Balderstone Mill. For boys employment included work at the mill, but also farm work. Jane Hall was the daughter of Robert Hall (ropemaker) and Jane Iddon. She was born in February 1868 and was therefore aged only eleven years eleven months when the certificate was signed.
She married George Allanson in 1900.

Courtesy of Mrs. Irene Walker (nee Allanson), grand-daughter of Jane Hall.

made by one of Her Majesty's Inspectors (HMI). Prior to 1876 inspectors were organised on denominational lines, with the churches having a say in the choice of inspectors, but in 1876 inspectors were re-organised by area. The HMI inspection at Trinity School of August 1876 provides an insight into the lessons then being taught and the success achieved

> The School has made very satisfactory progress during the past year. Order is good and the elementary subjects except spelling and composition in the fourth and fifth standards are now fairly accurate. Handwriting however wants care and style and the

> children should read with more expression and distinctness. The Class subjects of Grammar, Geography and sewing have been well prepared. Sewing deserves special praise. The accounts should be kept intelligibly. The last report cannot be found and does not seem to have been fully entered in the Log Book.

The entry in the log book 'Examination of Night School this evening' is confirmation of the previously mentioned anecdotal recollections of George Wylie Rigby. Unfortunately no further information is given, but the classes were almost certainly inter-denominational and not restricted to those adults who attended Holy Trinity Church.

In 1877 the school holidays were Easter Monday, a week at Whitsuntide, two weeks in August, a half day on November 5, and a week at Christmas. Playtime however did not figure prominently in the daily routine, as revealed by an entry in the school log of 5 September 1877, when Mr. Martin recorded that he 'Allowed the children a few minutes play on the [village] green this afternoon'. Restricted playtime was probably to compensate for the range of absences that interrupted the teaching schedule, as revealed by the following entries in the log book

Balderstone Mill

For over a hundred and fifty years (c1820–1980) the linen / cotton factory (from around 1866 known as Balderstone Mill) was a major employer of village labour. It stood diagonally across from Trinity School.

4 July 1876	A few of the children are away this week on account of Kirkham Club
14 July 1876	All the bigger children away this week, haymaking
27 April 1877	Some of the winter Scholars are beginning to leave school again

It was, however, the frequent epidemics and illnesses that caused the greatest disruption

13 April 1877	Whooping [cough] is very bad indeed amongst the children and has reduced the infants average 50 per cent
4 March 1878	Another of the scholars – Elizabeth Whittle – has died of typhoid fever. Three families are prevented from sending their children to school on account of that disease
8 Dec. 1879	The measles are very prevalent in the village and the average attendance is greatly reduced
22 Sept. 1881	Scarlet has broken out in the village and several children are kept at home suffering from it

Illness was not confined just to the children, and when a teacher was absent their place was often taken by one of the older and more capable children, as happened in May 1877 when 'Michael Coulborn taught throughout the week in place of Miss Martin'.

On 28 June 1878 the school was closed in the afternoon 'on account of a meeting to be held with regard to passing bye-laws (the previously mentioned School Attendance Committee) relating to the attendance of children at School'. Thereafter this bye-law appears to have been strictly enforced at Freckleton, and in December 1878 Thomas Rawcliffe was summoned before the magistrates for neglecting to send his child to school. He gave as his reason that 'he thought the schoolmistress was unable to teach the child'.[48]

In the same year (1878) the system of "half-timers" was introduced. Children under ten were debarred from employment in factories (Balderstone Mill was a major employer of labour in Freckleton at this time), and those under thirteen who were employed were under an obligation to attend school either one session each day (half-time) throughout the week, or one full day on alternate days. On 19 July 1878 Mr. Martin recorded in the log book that 'the factory inspector called today and enquired about the half-timers'.

The Elementary Education Act of 1880 made school attendance compulsory. And by 1881 the entire population of England was required to send its children to school until they were ten years of age, at which age a child could obtain their "certificate of proficiency" and become a "half-timer", but only if attendance had been satisfactory.

In May 1881 classes at Trinity School were arranged so that Mr. Martin taught the 1st and 4th Classes (Standards I, IV, V, and VI,); Miss Martin taught the 2nd Class (Standard III); Kate Noble, the niece of Mr. Martin who had joined the school as a pupil teacher in 1881, taught the 3rd Class (Standard II); the Infants were under the care of Elizabeth Richardson, a monitor.

The management of the school, despite Freckleton having been made an ecclesiastical parish seven years previously, still remained nominally under the control of the vicar of Warton and his churchwardens. By 1881 however, both Edward Myres, a solicitor who resided at Naze House, Freckleton, and his brother Thomas Harrison Myres, an architect who resided at Naze Cottage, Freckleton, had been appointed school managers.

Their father, Alderman John James Myres was a member of Preston Corporation from 1842 until his death in 1881. The Myres family played a significant role in the church life of Freckleton during the 1870s and 1880s, and at a sermon preached, in 1881, in memory of Alderman Myres, the Rev. Scott described him as 'a cordial helper in every movement that he originated for the use of the parish'.

On 5 December 1881 Thomas Harrison Myres wrote to the Charity Commissioners requesting that they agree to the management of Trinity School being transferred to the vicar of Freckleton and a 'committee of persons in the district of Freckleton'. He also re-affirmed that the school had been established 'for the education of the poor of Freckleton'.[49]

Mr. Myres added that the yearly income in the previous financial year (1880–1881), which had been used to provide the salaries for the Master, Mistress, and Pupil Teacher, and also repairs to the school and school house, had been £155 2s. 6d. consisting of

Government Grant	£81 18s 0d.
Contributions	£8 15s. 6d.
Collections at Church	£3 6s. 6d.
School Pence	£55 3s. 11d.
Other Sources }	
School Concerts }	£5 18s. 7d.

On 15 August 1882 the Charity Commissioners agreed that the vicar and churchwardens of Warton should no longer have any role in the running of the school. The school managers, who then assumed full responsibility for the management of Trinity School, were Rev. Scott, who, as the vicar of Freckleton, had to be chairman of all meetings at which he was present; William Moorhouse Martin, who in addition to being the schoolmaster was

also the churchwarden; and Robert Cookson, William Cookson, Robert Moon, Edward Myres, and Thomas Harrison Myres. The Charity Commissioners also stipulated that no person could be appointed master or mistress of the school who was not a member of the Church of England.[50]

Five months previously (March 1882) Mr. Martin had only recently returned to teaching duties having been absent from November 1880 due to debility following enteric fever. This absence of authority was probably one of the causes which, in September 1882, resulted in several parents being summoned before the School Attendance Committee on account of the irregular attendance of their children.

And after a further 'long illness' Mr. Martin resigned in October 1882. In the same month a temporary master, Mr. J. N. Herbert, was appointed. He served until 21 December the same year. Frustrated by the conditions he had found at the school his final entry in the log book paints a rather dismal picture

> I am sorry to say that during the two months I have had charge of this school I have been unable to get pens for the scholars to write with and there has not been, and I could not get, a drop of ink except about a quarter of a penny bottle, which stands on the Masters desk, to mark the registers with, also there is no arithmetic belonging to the school so that every sum has either to be marked before the school commences, or during the lesson, which of course takes up much time, which might be much more beneficially employed.

On the day the school broke up for the Christmas holidays Mr. Herbert's final act was distribute the gifts (toys and dolls) sent the previous day by Mrs. Fields of Lytham. The fact that these gifts came from a benefactor outside the village is probably due simply to Mrs. Fields' response to a request by Mr. Herbert. Nevertheless it is also an indication of the continuing underlying poverty present in the village.

Such circumstances must have been apparent for some time, and cannot have failed to concentrate the minds of the new school managers. One of their first acts was to appoint James Bramwell, a man with drive and determination, as the new master. It was a wise choice. Born in Preston he was aged twenty eight when he commenced duties on 8 January 1883.

Although there is evidence from other school log books that the masters wrote critical notes about the state of the school they had inherited, in order to limit any subsequent personal blame on them by H.M. Inspectors, it seems obvious that in 1883 Trinity School was in need of much attention.

In a detailed first day entry in the log book Mr. Bramwell confirmed what Mr. Herbert's had written on his last day at Trinity School, and also commented on the want of desks and the insufficient number of staff. He also made a complete inventory of school materials (books and maps). On the following day he noted that 'All work in Arith[metic], Dictation, Writing, and Geography [has] to be done on slates'.

Within four days of his appointment Mr. Bramwell had obtained two quarts of ink from Mr. Sowerbutts, the owner of Balderstone Mill, and had gone one evening to Kirkham but, unable to obtain any penholders, had continued to Preston where he obtained supplies. By 12 January he was able to report 'Exercise books bought up rather readily by the children. Home lessons a new feature here'.

In addition, and despite the improvements to the building only fifteen years earlier, the premises were still far from adequate. On 10 February Thomas Harrison Myres noted that 'the walls were damp and the drainage of the yards and urinal were defective'.

By April, 'after much delay', six desks, two blackboards, and two easels had arrived. Mr. Bramwell then turned his attention to employing suitable staff, and in August Miss Miles was appointed assistant mistress at a salary of £30 per annum. However, Mr. Bramwell had great difficulty in persuading able pupils to take up the post of pupil teacher, and in the same month he recorded that 'The boy Stanley Iddon, who had given the Master to understand he was desirous of becoming a pupil teacher, stated today that his mother wished him to assist at home in the farm work'.

The HMI report of 1883, although not blaming Mr. Bramwell, made several adverse comments concerning the level of attainment, and expressed concern at the lack of adequate accommodation. The Inspector concluded by recommending the grant but 'with great hesitation'.

In July 1883 the number of pupils was recorded as two hundred and twenty eight, of whom one hundred and twenty nine attended all week, forty one were half-timers, fifty two were "partial", and a further six were recorded as "not attending". But, as the Inspector had noted, the existing accommodation made perfect order and organisation impossible.

In addition to the HMI inspection the school was also subject to a "Diocesan Report in Religious Knowledge" (the then diocese being Manchester). In July 1883 an entry in the log book records that the inspector reported that 'This School exhibits a most marked improvement since it has passed under Mr Bramwell's care'.

It was however the HMI report that seems to have had the desired effect as the school managers immediately began fund raising activities. At their meeting in July 1884 it was resolved 'to collect the promised subscriptions, to solicit more assistance, and to begin building, to a plan submitted by Thomas Harrison Myres, when £120 had been put in the savings Bank, Preston'.

A month later plans of the proposed alterations were again submitted, with the tender for the work from 'Mr. Saul, Contractor of Preston'. And it was resolved 'to accept the tender and plans and that the building should be proceeded with as early as possible'.

Among those who subscribed was Newton Charity (the owners of Lower House Farm), who agreed in September 1884 that 'as Landowners in Freckleton the Trustees are prepared to give a donation of £25 towards the enlargement of Freckleton School should the same be done at a cost of not less than £200 and the plan be to the satisfaction of the Trustees'.[51] By 31 October work was almost completed, and Mr. Bramwell was able to record 'Workmen again engaged on the New room finishing plastering & whitewashing'.

Unfortunately, there are no known plans of this extension, but it can only have been the infants classroom that was subsequently destroyed in the air disaster of 1944. The room does not appear on plans of the school made in 1867, but does appear on a drawing of the school made in 1892.

Thus within two years Mr. Bramwell, together with the managers, had achieved an enlargement of the school that was necessary to meet the needs of an increasing population. In order to warm the schoolrooms fires were lit throughout the winter from mid-October onwards, and the parents of the children were asked to contribute towards the cost. Although there were cases in which parents refused to pay their share, most parents readily paid the annual 6d charge.

Mr. Bramwell was also making progress in raising the educational standards. He laid great emphasis on discipline and respect, and late attendance and insubordination could result in a child being sent home accompanied by a teacher. In one incident, that began in November 1884 and continued through to February 1885, Mr. Bramwell was adamant 'that on every fine day' the children of two families 'were to come [to school] without stable and shippon dirt about their shoes and trousers'.

With only relatively short breaks between each term the principal annual social event for the pupils was Club Day. Events to mark special events in the life of the nation, and the prospect of special treats, must therefore have been anticipated with great excitement.

On Saturday 25 June 1887 festivities were held to mark the Golden Jubilee of Queen Victoria. During the afternoon 'about 500 medals (the gifts of H. E. Sowerbutts, Esq, the owner of Balderstone Mill) were distributed amongst the scholars by Messrs. Bramwell and Taylor'.[52] These medals were given not only to present pupils but, as Mr. Bramwell noted in the log book, 'to scholars past and present'. In the late afternoon 'at the National School room about 80 folks over sixty, and over 300 children were treated to a substantial

Trinity School early twentieth century
An early twentieth century view of Trinity School and original schoolhouse (left). The infants classroom on the east side of the school (nearest to the schoolhouse) was added in 1884. It was this classroom that was destroyed in the 1944 air disaster. The schoolhouse, then occupied by the school caretaker, was also damaged beyond repair.
Copyright not known.

tea'. In the evening a concert was given in the school room 'before an audience principally of children'.[53]

The subscribers who met the cost of the event were named as Rev. Walter Scott, H. E. Sowerbutts, Esq, the managers of the school, and 'other friends'. Mr. Bramwell was named as the 'prime mover in the affair who carried out all the arrangements so well'.[54]

The reality of school life, however, soon returned, and in October 1887 Mr. Bramwell was expressing concern over the lack of enforcement relating to half-timers. He noted, in the log book, that 'Several children have lately obtained half-time certificates under the pretence of working at the Mill, but have either not attended or only occasionally done so. Many children seen playing in the street during School hours'.

Although great emphasis was placed on discipline Mr. Bramwell also ensured that his staff did not ill-treat the pupils. When, in September 1887, Mrs. C. Whittle complained of Miss Clayton striking her child Ellen, Mr. Bramwell entered in the log book 'This is not the first occasion a complaint has been made of this teacher, and the Master has cautioned her respecting striking the children'.

Despite this, and other incidents, Miss Clayton, who had been appointed in December 1885, remained at the school until November 1894. She returned in January 1905, and included in her subjects was botany. These were outdoor classes where 'each pupil was awarded a "G for good" if a new flower was found, with twenty "Gs" earning a pupil a penny'.[55] Miss Clayton finally retired in September 1939 aged 72, having taught at Trinity School for a total of forty three years seven months.

Mr. Bramwell's own long term commitment to Freckleton was demonstrated in

1888. Even though the school managers refused to extend the schoolmasters house, 'from want of funds and consideration of future requirements', he was allowed to sub-let the property. He then moved to Ivanhoe, Green Lane, where he was recorded on the 1891 census together with his wife, six daughters, and two sons.

Another critical HMI report in 1890 resulted in several staff changes, including the appointment of Mr. Bramwell's brother, Edward, as assistant master. Efforts were also made to extend the range of subjects taught. Further demands were placed on the staff following the passing of another Elementary Education Act in August 1891. This Act introduced fee grants, the conditions of which were

> After the commencement of this Act, there shall be paid, out of moneys provided by Parliament, and at such times and in such manner as may be determined by regulations of the Education Department, a grant in aid of the cost of elementary education in England and Wales at the rate of ten shillings a year for each child of the number of children over three and under fifteen years of age in average attendance at any public elementary school in England and Wales (not being an evening school) the managers of which are willing to receive the same, and in which the Education Department are satisfied that the regulations as to fees are in accordance with the conditions in this Act

At a meeting of the school managers held on 1 September 1891 it was unanimously resolved that the school pence be abolished, and the school declared free, but that the pupils pay for stationery and firing as before. A general wish was expressed that, 'in order to enable the managers to carry on the school as in its past efficient state, friends, and especially the parents of the children, will contribute handsomely to make up any deficiency that may occur in consequence of the change in the law'.[56]

Up to that date most parents in Freckleton appear to have been able to pay the fee themselves, but even a month before the abolition at least two pupils had had to have their fees paid by the Poor Law guardians.

Two immediate consequences of the 1891 Act are revealed by an entry in the log book of 24 September when Mr. Bramwell recorded that ' Several children under 3 years of age sent to school now it is free, many of the older scholars rather irregular making 7, 8 or 9 attendances instead of 10 as formerly'.

Additional pressure must have been placed on Mr. Bramwell when the age of compulsory attendance was further increased to eleven in 1893, and to twelve in 1899. In the latter year half-time exemption could be claimed at twelve years of age subject to five years of good attendance, as was the case for full exemption at thirteen years.

Ill-health also continued to affect attendance, and every year there are entries in the log book recording the absence of the children due to various ailments. Other causes were, in many instances, the same as those encountered by Mr. Martin twenty years earlier. Throughout the 1890s, during the months of June and July, there were always several pupils absent all week working in the hay fields. Other causes of absence included that of Thomas Singleton who, in May 1892, was reported as being 'employed illegally in a brick yard', and in June 1896 George Helm was 'illegally employed on Freckleton Marsh'.

Even attempts by the attendance officer to improve matters were often thwarted, as on 20 February 1894 when, after cautioning a few irregulars, he received no help from those present when he asked for the names of any children of five years of age not yet attending school. Occasionally the children received an unexpected holiday, as in 1897 when the school was closed from 18 June to 23 June for the celebration of Queen Victoria's Diamond Jubilee.

Throughout the 1890s there appears to have been a night school for recent school leavers, and (possibly) adults. In November 1890 the night school opened with an attendance of fifty, of whom twenty one took an examination the following March, though in what subjects is not recorded.

In 1899 an entry in the log book recorded that 'the Committee on Technical Education would make no grant this year towards a Night School or Continuation Class', and Mr. Bramwell was advised 'not to trouble about a Class for the coming year'. However the decision must have been reversed because in October 1900 the H.M. Inspector 'visited the Evening Continuation Class'.

Improvements to the school during the 1890s included the installation of a hot water heating system, used for the first time in January 1892, and new water closets approved in August 1893. Nevertheless, despite all efforts at improvement, the HMI report of 1898 made depressing reading when the inspector stated

> The rooms are inconvenient, not overclean, badly ventilated and not particularly cheerful. The cloak rooms are inadequate. An additional Class-room would mitigate the inconvenience, though possibly a new Infant school would be a more economical remedy in the end

In order to remedy the situation the managers once more began fund raising for school improvements, and money was obtained by means of appeals and sales of work. In 1901 the school was enlarged at a cost of £400. But even after the enlargement fund raising continued and, in February 1902, the Rev. Edward Hack (vicar of Freckleton 1892–1917) wrote to Newton Charity to request a donation as the school was 'in debt'.[57]

At the same time that these fund raising events were taking place Parliament

James Bramwell (headmaster) and Class of 1896
On 1 May 1896 Mr. Devey, a Preston photographer, came to Freckleton and photographed the pupils at Trinity School in five groups. This group photograph also includes James Bramwell, who was headmaster from 1883 to 1913. The only pupils who have been identified are Robert Richardson (Back Row 5th left), Margaret Hunter (Third Row 7th left), and Mary Ellen Seed (Third Row 1st right – behind Mr. Bramwell)

Courtesy of Mrs. Kitty Garlick (nee Kirby), who also identified the pupils.

passed the 1902 Education Act which radically reorganised the administration of education at local level. The Act abolished school boards in England and Wales, and all elementary schools were placed in the hands of local education authorities under the control of the county and county borough councils. The Act, for the first time, also made provision for secondary and technical education. Councils were encouraged, though not compelled, to subsidise existing grammar schools and to provide free places for "working-class" children.

In their report for 1903/03 the Charity Commissioners noted that 'in each of the last 3 years donations of £10 have been made [by Newton Charity] to Freckleton School'. These donations, together with other fund raising events, enabled the Rev.Hack, in 1905, to report to the bishop of Manchester 'We have spent in recent years about £600 & now we have more than sufficient accommodation'. In 1908 the H.M. Inspector recommended the removal of the gallery, and that a supply of some modern desks 'should be proceeded with at the earliest opportunity'.

At the beginning of the twentieth century class subjects were English grammar and geography for all standards, history from reading lessons in Standards III to VI, elementary subjects (the 3 R's) for all in the school. In addition there was drawing for boys; needlework for all girls and also boys in the infant's class; and singing and physical exercises. In 1906 Norman Cardwell was successful in gaining a scholarship at Kirkham Grammar School, and was placed first among the successful candidates.

However, for the majority of pupils progress into higher education remained elusive. Conversely, irregular attendance, occasioned by social and domestic "requirements", was an ever present problem. In February 1906 Mr. Bramwell noted that Mr. William Mathew Buck, the school attendance officer, (who prior to his appointment in 1895 had been butler to the Birley family at Clifton Hall) 'finding other schools closed for Shrove Tuesday called here this afternoon and cautioned a few children about irregular attendance'.

In 1909, and for several years afterwards, the school was visited by Sergeant Major Wright from Fulwood, who inspected the children carrying out their

REV. EDWARD HACK AND MISS AGNES TODD AND CLASS OF 1896
Rev. Edward John Hack (vicar of Freckleton 1892–1917) was closely involved in the day to day running of the school. This photograph appears to be the infants class whose teacher was Miss Agnes Todd. The only pupil who can be identified is Annie Wray Rigby (Third Row 1st left), the daughter of George Wylie Rigby and Elizabeth Sumner.

Courtesy of Mrs. Margaret Hall (nee Bannister), who also identified Annie Wray Rigby.

William Matthew Buck – School Attendance Officer
The role of the school attendance officer was to ensure that pupils made regular attendance, including the "half-timers" who worked at Balderstone Mill. Prior to his appointment in 1895 William Matthew Buck had been butler to the Birley family at Clifton Hall. He continued to be the school attendance officer until at least 1924.
Courtesy of Mrs. Doris Marshall Whalley per Alan Watkinson, great-grandson of William Matthew Buck.

"P.E." exercises. On his visit in 1913 he expressed himself satisfied that the children knew the exercises but considered that 'more vigour should be put into them'. Three years earlier the range in subjects had been extended, and fifteen girls and nine boys were offered external classes in cookery and woodwork at Kirkham.

By 1910, in addition to the occasional "entertainments" held at the school, the children enjoyed longer holidays than had their parents, including from 1908 a half day holiday for Empire Day. They were also given a holiday on special occasions, as in May 1902 when the school closed for a week for the coronation of King Edward VII, and for a further week in September for the Preston Guild Merchant. In 1911 a one day holiday was granted for the coronation of King George V, and in July 1913 the children were taken to Lytham for the visit of the King and Queen.

Conditions within the school were improved in 1911 with the removal of the gallery, and the provision of some dual desks. In September 1913 Mr. Bramwell fell from a ladder whilst winding the school clock, and sustained a serious injury to his right foot. Throughout the remainder of 1913, and most of 1914, he encountered severe difficulty in walking, and Richard Mason (born 1900) recalled pushing Mr. Bramwell to school in a wheelchair.[58]

Mr. Bramwell resigned as master in November 1914 after thirty years dedicated service to Trinity School. He was, and still is, the longest serving (head) master of the school. The present day Bramwell Close is named after him in recognition of his service to the village.

CHAPTER FOUR

The inter-war years

James Bramwell was succeeded as headmaster by John (Jack) Winchester on 1 December 1914. Mr. Winchester was born at Newton with Scales in 1886, and his teacher training was at Sheffield University from 1905 to 1907. He does not appear to have ever resided in Freckleton, but cycled to school from his home in Marsden Street, Kirkham. A former Preston North End footballer, Mr. Winchester established the first school football team and 'pupils saved pennies for several weeks in order to buy strip and boots'.[59]

On 11 January 1915 Mr. Winchester received the report made by the H.M. Inspector in December 1914. The inspector noted that during the previous fourteen months the school 'had passed through a trying time' due to the prolonged illness and eventual resignation of Mr. Bramwell.

In addition to a wide range of suggested recommendations for the incoming headmaster to implement, the H.M. Inspector also pointed out to the managers that 'According to the temperature charts the heating of the rooms is still unsatisfactory; the recent improvements have not been entirely successful'. It was also recommended that 'the offices (toilets) should be flushed more frequently'.

Due to restrictions following the outbreak of World War I the school was without heating fuel by October 1915, and in the winter of 1915–16 and succeeding wartime winters school hours were adjusted to comply with the lighting restriction order. Mr. Winchester himself had to attend several military medical boards before being considered fit only for sedentary duties.

In October 1916 five boys aged twelve years, in common with pupils elsewhere, were granted permission to be absent to gather potatoes, a task repeated by other boys, and girls, in 1917 and 1918. In addition 'Socks & Mittens knit by girls for soldier comforts [were] distributed to those whose fathers or brothers were serving in France'.

The school log books also record the gathering of blackberries which, due to the shortage of fruit would have been an important supplement to the diet of the children and their parents. And in May 1917, at the request of the Lancashire Education Committee, 'the lessons were devised with a view to instruction on Food Economy'. In the same year a War Savings Committee was formed.

A more unusual war effort is recalled from a log book entry in October 1917 'Chestnuts collected by children brought to school preparatory to being forwarded to the Director of Propellant Supplies – weight collected about 1 cwt'. The reason for this particular war effort was that during World War I chestnuts were used for the production of acetone, which in turn was needed to produce cordite, the smokeless powder used as a propellant in small arms ammunition and artillery.

Both before and throughout the war ill-health continued to be a cause for concern, and the school was often closed due to outbreaks of diphtheria, smallpox, measles, and scarlet fever. Although the regular medical inspections, which began in 1913, were evidence of increasing awareness of the need to combat these potentially fatal diseases, it was not always possible to prevent frequent serious outbreaks. There was a particularly serious outbreak of mumps in autumn 1916, as revealed by the following entries in the school log book

7 September	Cases of Mumps spreading rapidly – nine actually suffering from disease & twelve living in infected houses absent
22 September	Dr. Court Medical Officer visits school concerning Infectious Diseases ... Orders closing of school for fortnight
7 October	School re-opens after closure of epidemic – extremely poor attendance – 127 absentees. Report to Medical Officer who orders closure for another fortnight.
21 October	School re-opens – poor attendance – 83 absentees. Report to Medical Officer who advises continuance [of school].

Illness was also the reason why it was not possible to celebrate Armistice Day in November 1918. The school had been closed since 30 October on the orders of the medical officer due to an outbreak of influenza, and did not re-open until 9 December. A Peace Holiday, however, was held in September 1919.

During his eight years at Freckleton Mr. Winchester added both swimming and nature study to the school curriculum. Academic standards continued to improve and, for example, in July 1915 Thomas Mason of Kirkham Road and Henry Allanson of Clitheroes Lane both obtained a foundation scholarship at Kirkham Grammar School. An achievement repeated by James Rawstrone in July the following year.

In July 1918 Elizabeth Rigby left Trinity School to attend Park School, Preston, and a month later the governors of Kirkham Grammar School advised Mr. Winchester that a number of exhibitions (bursaries), value about £13 10s 0d, at Park School, Preston or the Secondary School, Blackpool would be open for girls attending elementary schools in the 'Ancient Parish of Kirkham'. In the same year a further Education Act was passed which raised the school leaving age from twelve to fourteen.

Mr. Winchester relinquished his duties as headmaster in January 1921 following his appointment at Poulton C of E School, and was succeeded by Edward Cross Rigby. Mr. Rigby was born at Preston in 1888, and his teacher training was at Chester College from 1910 to 1912. In 1922 he was elected to Freckleton Parish Council, but in 1923, following his appointment at Prestwich C of E School, he resigned as headmaster at Freckleton.

Mr. Rigby was succeeded by John William Platts. Born at Penwortham in

John Winchester (headmaster) and Class of c1917
Back Row (L–R): Bill Hunter, Frank Scott, Jimmy Carr, Thomas Wignall, Not known, Thomas Harrison, John Whittle, Norman Garstang
Middle Row (L–R): Lizzie Rigby, Lizzie Whittle, Rebecca Carr, Eleanor Iddon, Margaret Wharton, Madge Richardson, Edith Porter, Annie Kirby, Gladys Rigby, Mr. Winchester
Front Row (L–R): Nellie Wilson, Robina Cook, Alice Banks, Alice Rayton, Mary Iddon, Lena Banks, Eleanor Swan, Margaret Brade, A. Cumpstey ?

Courtesy of Mrs. Drena Crone (nee Anyon). Pupils identified (source not known) on document associated with photograph provided by Mrs. Crone.

John Winchester (headmaster) and Class of c1920
Back Row (L–R): Not known, Tom Parkinson, Isaac Whittle, Harold Cardwell, George Helm, Billy Ibbison, John Thomas Rawstrone, John Battersby, Bill Armstrong
Third Row (L–R): Mr. Winchester, Henry Barlow, Annie Iddon, May Butcher, Alice Norris, Jane Salthouse, Maggie Cardwell, Mary Whiteside, Rose Singleton, John Rawstrone, Miss Edith Clayton
Second Row (L–R): Nellie Sumner, Kitty Whiteside, Bell Coulburn, Fanny Marquis, Edith Banks, Katy Greenwood, Lizzie Rawstrone, Mary Richardson
Front Row (L–R): Tom Eastham, Rimmer Iddon, Reggie Brade, Robert Hunter, John Worthington, Tom Pye, Robert Dewhurst
Miss Clayton taught at Trinity School for a total of forty three years – 1885 to 1894 and 1905 to 1939

Courtesy of Mrs. Margaret Hall (nee Bannister), who also recorded the names of the pupils per the late Mrs. Ann Bennett (nee Hull), the late Mrs. Edna Mason (nee Rawstrone), and the late Mrs. Elsie Sandford (nee Bee).

1885, Mr. Platts was assistant master at Cop Lane School, Penwortham, from 1904 to 1906. His teacher training was at Exeter College from 1906 to 1908. He was then an assistant master at Adlington National School from 1908 to 1909, and at St. Chrysostom's Church of England School, Everton, from 1909 to 1919. This latter appointment was interrupted by military service, when, during World War I, he was a prisoner of war. Following further appointments, as a first assistant master at two other Liverpool schools, he was appointed headmaster at Freckleton in 1923.

At the time of Mr. Platt's appointment the need for a new school was clearly apparent. Following the purchase of additional land in 1922 and 1924 further improvements were carried out to the building. However, and in spite of improved conditions, ill health continued to be a feature of the school year, and outbreaks of measles, scarlet fever, and influenza caused the school to be closed on a regular basis.

The practice of half-time also continued with many pupils, on attaining the age of thirteen years, attending half a day at school and half a day at Balderstone Mill, alternating weekly mornings and afternoons. At the age of fourteen pupils left school to work full-time.[60] Pupils were also still required to provide funds towards the heating of the school, and, each week, had to take either a penny or a lump of coal.[61]

In the early part of 1925 there was considerable canvassing in the village for support to forward a request to Lancashire County Council to provide a council school. On 23 February a letter was presented to Freckleton Parish Council by those ratepayers in favour of a council school. A month later a further letter from the ratepayers claimed the privilege of an 'undenominational school', following which the parish council voted six to two in favour of such a school.

It was a somewhat fractious affair, and it prompted the Rev. Richard Hayward (vicar of Freckleton 1922–1929) to write an article in the parish magazine, which was also reproduced in the *Lancashire Daily Post*.[62] In his article Rev. Hayward vigorously defended the role Trinity School had played in the life of the village, pointing out that 'some of the older generation would not have been able to read or write but for our Church school'. As we shall see, the debate was to presage the events that followed the air disaster of 1944.

Whilst the inadequacy of the school premises was highlighted in the HMI inspection of 14 May 1925, the report also noted the creditable work that had been achieved

> The numbers in attendance have increased and there are now six classes in four rooms. Notwithstanding the crowded conditions in the two larger rooms, each with two classes, and the extent to which continuity of work has been interrupted during the past year by closure on account of epidemic, and by absence of staff through sickness, much creditable work has been done and a fairly good standard is attained generally

The report was sufficient to enable the Lancashire Elementary Education Sub-committee to write to the parish council and inform them that 'in view

Above Miss Jane Elizabeth Hall and Class of c1922
Jane Elizabeth Hall was appointed Infants Mistress in September 1900.
From May to December 1914, during the enforced absence of James Bramwell, she was appointed acting headteacher. She resigned in 1922.
The only pupil that can be identified is Elizabeth (Cissie) Hall (second row 6th left – next to Miss Hall) who was born in 1912. She first attended school on 1 May 1917.

Courtesy of David Kirby. Cissie Hall identified by Michael Lancaster (her son).

Football Team 1922/3

The earliest known photograph of a school football team. The captain is Henry Barlow (centre, middle row). His brother, Charlie Barlow, is on the right facing side of the front row. The first school football team was established by John Winchester, headmaster from 1914 to 1920, and who was a former Preston North End player.

School Archives. Pupils identified by Mrs. Elsie Dollin, the daughter of Henry Barlow.

Left Edward Rigby (headmaster) and Class of c1922

Back Row (L–R): Harold Cardwell, George Helm, Herbert Butler, John Worthington, George Rhodes, Billy Ibbison, Teddy Butcher, Tom Eastham, John Battersby

Third Row (L–R): , Madge Whittle, Annie Threlfall Mary Richardson, Mary Whiteside, Maggie Rawstrone, Annie Cartmell Alice Norris, Betty Butcher, Kitty Whiteside

Second Row (L–R): Grace Cottam (against window), Fanny Marquis, Edna Barlow, Hannah Brown, Maggie Whiteside, Lizzie Eastham, Mr. Rigby, Nellie Whiteside, Edith Banks, Katy Greenwood, Lizzie Rawstrone (against wall)

Front Row (L–R): Robert Hunter, Ralph Hull, John Garstang, Rimmer Iddon, Madge Pye, Grace Hankinson, Robert Dewhurst, Tom Pye, Not known, – Worthington, George Lonsdale, Bill Ramshead

Courtesy of Mrs. Margaret Hall (nee Bannister), who also provided the names of the pupils per the late Mrs. Ann Bennett (nee Hull), the late Mrs. Edna Mason (nee Rawstrone), and the late Mrs. Elsie Sandford (nee Bee).

Miss M. Fenton and Class of c1924

Back Row (L–R): Albert Wray, Robert Rawstrone, Sydney Whittle, Jack Rawstrone Stanley Hamer, Tom Porter, Harry Salthouse, Rigby Worthington, Richard Spencer, Jack Wilson, Miss Fenton

Front Row (L–R): Lizzie Eastham (1), Daisy Fisher, Agnes Whittle, Clarice Dickinson, Lizzie Eastham (2), Dolly Threlfall, Maggie Coulton, Lizzie Sudell, Betsy Kirby

Courtesy of Mrs. Ann Carnall (nee Fisher) – photo from collection of her late father Jack Fisher. Pupils identified by Mrs. Nellie Mason (nee Rigby).

Opposite School Plans – 1924

Plans made in 1924 for the extension of the boys cloakroom. In May 1925 the inadequacy of the school premises was highlighted in the H.M. Inspectors report . By this date there were six classes in four rooms. The two larger rooms each had two classes. In October 1925 an inquiry was held to discuss the need 'for a new school'.

Courtesy of Archives Service Manager, Lancashire Archives – ref PR3216/11/4.

Overleaf School Timetable 1930

The detailed planning required to ensure the smooth running of a varied curriculum is evident in the timetable prepared by John William Platts in August 1930.

School Archives. Photograph by Brian Hudson.

of the favourable report on the condition of the C of E school & the heavy building programme of the Education Committee the Local committee were at present unable to make any recommendation for a Council School'.[63]

However, all this notwithstanding, it would appear that pressure was maintained on the county council, and on 15 October 1925 the building was inspected by the Director of Education for Lancashire and the Secretary for Elementary Education. Following the inspection the Director invited Mr. Platts to an inquiry held at the Hodgson Institute (now the site of the Village Memorial Hall) to discuss the 'need for a new school'.

No further action, however, appears to have been taken and four years later an entry in the school log book records that the school was 'wired for electricity in conformity with a specification prepared by the County Architects Department. An electric cooker for heating children's dinners has been installed, and the Horlick's Cooker has been converted for electric current. During the first fortnight of the holidays an electrical exhibition arranged by Lytham St Anne's Corporation was held in the school'.

During the inter-war years patriotism played a significant role in school life, and Armistice Day (11 November) was commemorated with a service, whilst Empire Day (24 May) was celebrated with a pageant in which the pupils themselves participated. On 28 June 1927 the pupils assembled in the school

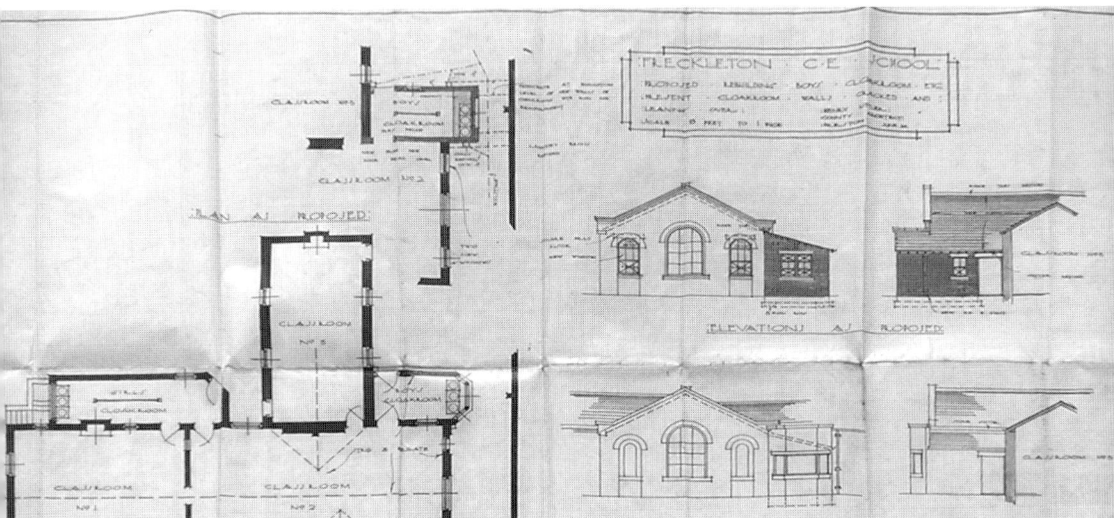

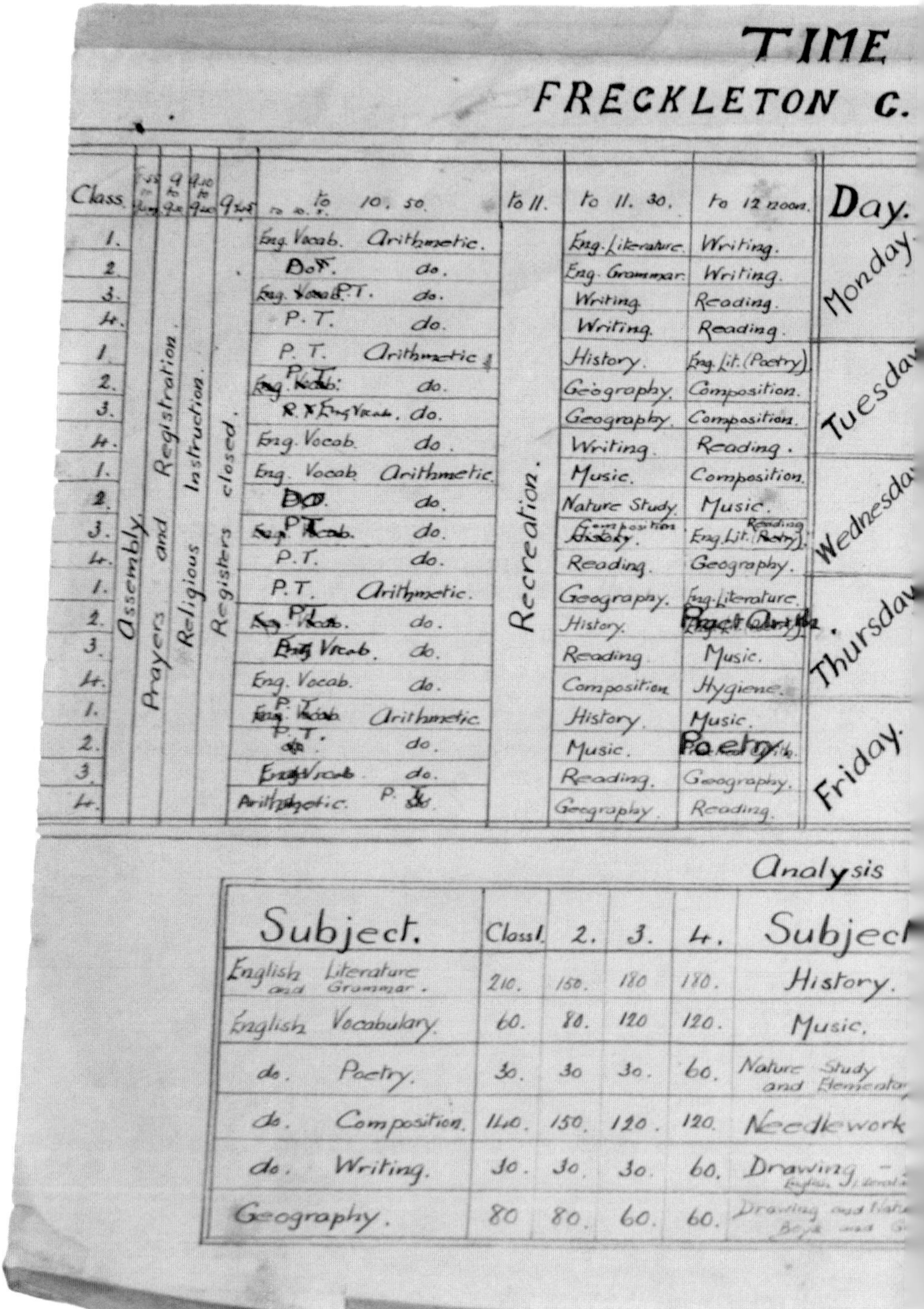

TIME

FRECKLETON C.

Class	8.55 to 9	9 to 9.10	9.10 to 9.[illegible]	9.15 to 10.[illegible]	to 10.50	to 11.	to 11.30.	to 12 noon.	Day.
1.	Assembly.	Prayers and Registration.	Religious Instruction.	Eng. Vocab.	Arithmetic.	Recreation.	Eng. Literature.	Writing.	Monday.
2.				(Do.)	do.		Eng. Grammar.	Writing.	
3.				Eng. Vocab. P.T.	do.		Writing.	Reading.	
4.				P.T.	do.		Writing.	Reading.	
1.				P.T.	Arithmetic.		History.	Eng. Lit. (Poetry).	Tuesday.
2.				P.T. (Eng. Vocab.)	do.		Geography.	Composition.	
3.				R.T. Eng. Vocab.	do.		Geography.	Composition.	
4.				Eng. Vocab.	do.		Writing.	Reading.	
1.			Registers closed.	Eng. Vocab.	Arithmetic.		Music.	Composition.	Wednesday.
2.				(Do.)	do.		Nature Study.	Music.	
3.				P.T. (Eng. Vocab.)	do.		Composition (History).	Reading (Eng. Lit. (Poetry)).	
4.				P.T.	do.		Reading.	Geography.	
1.				P.T.	Arithmetic.		Geography.	Eng. Literature.	Thursday.
2.				P.T. (Eng. Vocab.)	do.		History.	Pract. Arith.	
3.				Eng. Vocab.	do.		Reading.	Music.	
4.				Eng. Vocab.	do.		Composition.	Hygiene.	
1.				P.T. (Eng. Vocab.)	Arithmetic.		History.	Music.	Friday.
2.				P.T.	do.		Music.	Poetry.	
3.				Eng. Vocab.	do.		Reading.	Geography.	
4.				Arithmetic.	P.T.		Geography.	Reading.	

Analysis

Subject.	Class 1.	2.	3.	4.	Subject
English Literature and Grammar.	210.	150.	180	180.	History.
English Vocabulary.	60.	80.	120	120.	Music.
do. Poetry.	30.	30	30.	60.	Nature Study and Elementary
do. Composition.	140.	150.	120.	120.	Needlework
do. Writing.	30.	30.	30.	60.	Drawing – English Literature
Geography.	80	80.	60.	60.	Drawing and Nature, Boys and

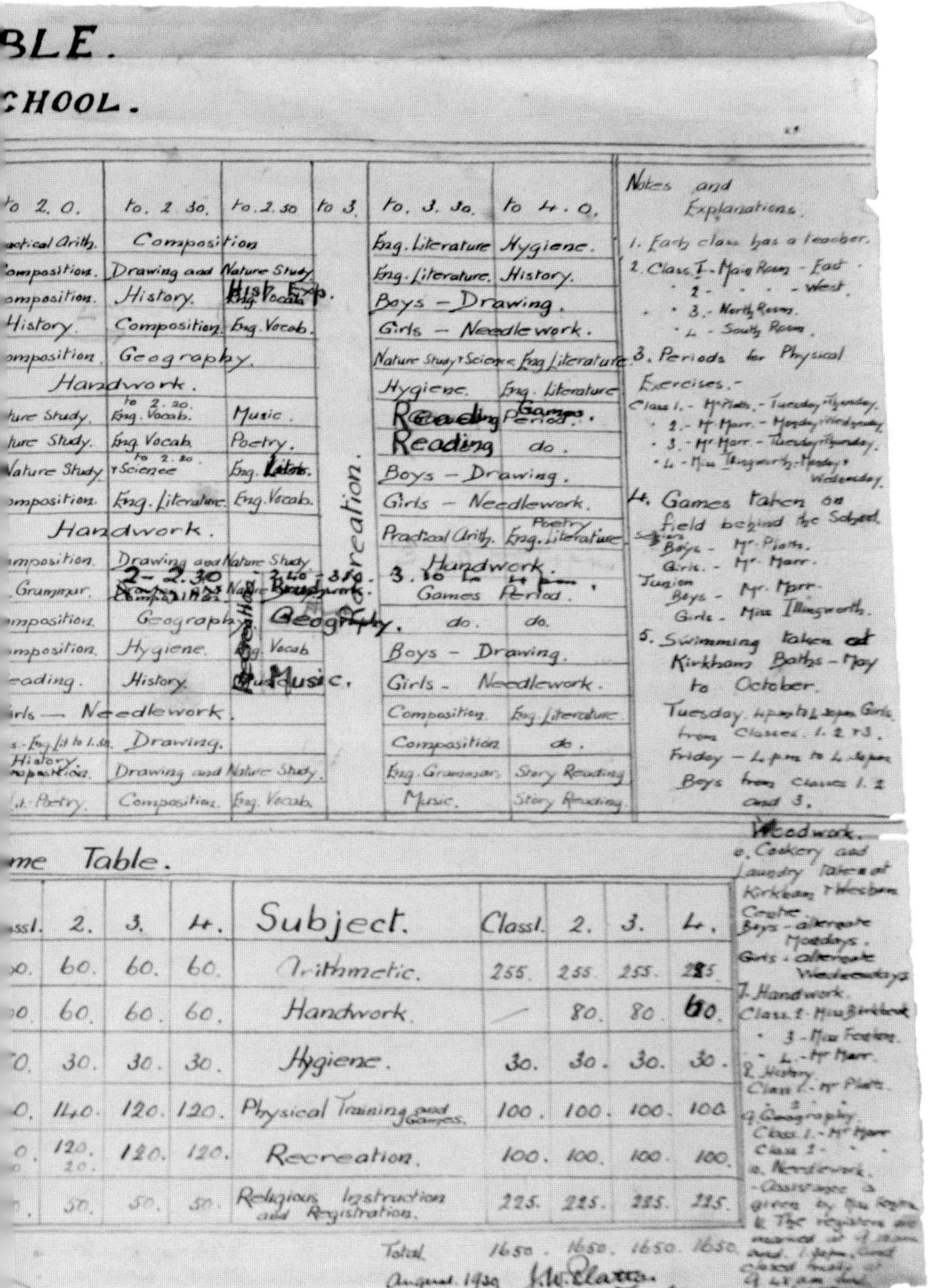
...BLE.

...CHOOL.

...to 2.0.	to 2.30.	to 2.50	to 3.	to 3.30.	to 4.0.
...ctical Arith.	Composition		Recreation.	Eng. Literature	Hygiene.
Composition.	Drawing and Nature Study			Eng. Literature.	History.
...omposition.	History.	Hist. Exp. / Eng. Vocab.		Boys – Drawing.	
History.	Composition.	Eng. Vocab.		Girls – Needlework.	
...omposition.	Geography.			Nature Study + Science	Eng. Literature
Handwork.				Hygiene.	Eng. Literature
...ture Study.	to 2.20. Eng. Vocab.	Music.		Reading	Games Period.
...ture Study.	Eng. Vocab.	Poetry.		Reading	do.
Nature Study	to 2.20. + Science	Eng. Liter.		Boys – Drawing.	
...omposition.	Eng. Literature.	Eng. Vocab.		Girls – Needlework.	
Handwork.				Practical Arith.	Poetry Eng. Literature
...mposition.	Drawing and Nature Study			Handwork.	
... Grammar.	2–2.30 Composition	Nature Study 2.40–3.10		3. to [illegible] Games Period.	
...mposition.	Geography	Geography.		do.	do.
...mposition.	Hygiene.	Eng. Vocab		Boys – Drawing.	
...eading.	History.	Music.		Girls – Needlework.	
...irls — Needlework.				Composition.	Eng. Literature.
...s.-Eng. Lit to 1.50	Drawing.			Composition	do.
History / ...mposition.	Drawing and Nature Study			Eng. Grammar	Story Reading
...Lit. Poetry.	Composition.	Eng. Vocab.		Music.	Story Reading

Notes and Explanations.

1. Each class has a teacher.
2. Class I – Main Room – East. 2 – – West. 3. – North Room. 4 – South Room.
3. Periods for Physical Exercises.– Class 1. – Mr Platts – Tuesday Thursday. 2. – Mr Marr – Monday Wednesday. 3. – Mr Marr – Tuesday Thursday. 4 – Miss Illingworth – Monday Wednesday.
4. Games taken on field behind the School. Senior Boys – Mr Platts. Girls – Mr Marr. Junior Boys – Mr Marr. Girls – Miss Illingworth.
5. Swimming taken at Kirkham Baths – May to October. Tuesday 4 p.m. to 4.30 p.m. Girls from Classes 1. 2 + 3. Friday – 4 p.m. to 4.30 p.m. Boys from Classes 1. 2 and 3.
6. Woodwork, Cookery and Laundry taken at Kirkham + Wesham Centre. Boys – alternate Mondays. Girls – alternate Wednesdays.
7. Handwork. Class 2 – Miss Birkbeck. 3 – Miss Foster. 4 – Mr Marr.
8. History. Class 2 – Mr Platts.
9. Geography. Class 1. – Mr Marr. Class 2 – " "
10. Needlework. – Assistance is given by [illegible]
11. The registers are marked at 9 a.m. and 1.30 p.m. and closed finally at 9.45 a.m. and 1.45 p.m.

...me Table.

Class 1.	2.	3.	4.	Subject.	Class 1.	2.	3.	4.
...0.	60.	60.	60.	Arithmetic.	255.	255.	255.	255.
...0	60.	60.	60.	Handwork.	—	80.	80	60.
...0.	30.	30.	30.	Hygiene.	30.	30.	30.	30.
...0.	140.	120.	120.	Physical Training and Games.	100.	100.	100.	100.
...0.	120. 20.	120.	120.	Recreation.	100.	100.	100.	100.
...	50.	50.	50.	Religious Instruction and Registration.	225.	225.	225.	225.
				Total	1650.	1650.	1650.	1650.

August 1930 [illegible] Head Teacher.

Mr. Robinson and Class of c1933/4
Back Row (L–R): Jack Whiteside, Jim Snape, Bob Carter, John Gornall, Sydney Hodgson, Reggie Townsend, Harry Whittle
Fourth Row (L–R): Charlotte Whittle, Tommy Allanson, Denis Clarke, John Williamson, Ralph Hall, Cyril Cadwallader, Jim Rhodes, John Butler
Third Row (L–R): Edie Greenwood, Muriel Rothwell, Betty Brown, Connie Threlfall, Molly Shannon, Bessie Whiteside, Jenny Rhodes, Jane Williamson, Joyce Wilson, Mr. Robinson
Second Row (L–R): Phyllis Worthington, Ethel Hewitt, Doris Ashton, Margaret Wignall, Doris Archer, Lena Banks, Evelyn Threlfall, Jennie Hall
Front Row (L–R): Bernard Cartmell, John Hall, Frank Buck, Norman Taylor, John Bonney, Joe Whiteside
Jennie Hall (second row) returned to the school as a teacher and was killed in the 1944 air disaster.
Copy of original photograph courtesy of Harry Whittle, who also identified the pupils.

yard at 3pm to see the Prince of Wales (later King Edward VIII) pass through the village.

In 1928 the school was divided into four "houses" – 'Balderstone', 'Hillock', 'Marsh', and 'Naze' – each with its own captain, vice-captain, and secretary. On 27 August 1934 Ernest Iddon, 'an old boy of the school', presented a silver shield engraved with the name of the school and mounted on an oak base. The shield was presented to the "house" 'which through application to work and merit proves the best house in any year'.

The school curriculum was also changing. One particular innovative exercise took place in June 1931 when, following a letter to Mr. Platts for information required by the Land Utilization Survey of Great Britain, the 'senior scholars' undertook the completion of Ordnance Survey Maps showing the local distribution of cultivated, pasture, woodland, and waste land. By this date parents were invited to visit the school and witness the classes at work, and school outings to London, Liverpool, and Chester were undertaken.

Events of national and international importance also featured in the daily life of the school. On 2 February 1932 Mr. Platts read out a letter, received from the President of the Board of Education, about the Disarmament Conference which opened at Geneva the same day. No doubt influenced by his own

Miss D. Illingworth and Class of 1934
Back Row (L–R): Tom Helm, Richard Worthington, Harry Bee, David Marquis, Not known, Robert Gornall, Jim Dickinson
Middle Row (L–R): Miss Illingworth, Belle Hall, Jenny Brown, Pearl Whittle, Doreen Bickerstaffe, Eileen Sandford, Phyllis Walker, Sylvia Allanson, Dorothy Whiteside
Front Row (L–R): Mervyn Clarke, Connie Fisher, Reggie Rawstrone, Joyce Haslam, Jackie Hough, Margaret Fisher, Richard Iddon, Lily Winchester, Eileen Hough
Courtesy of Richard Iddon. Pupils identified by Richard Iddon, Mrs. Kitty Garlick (nee Kirby), Mrs. Margaret Hall (nee Bannister), and Mrs. Eileen Woods (nee Hough)

John William Platts (headmaster) and Class of c1936 (Standard 6)
Back Row (L–R): Lilian Snape, Joyce Webster, Lena Banks, Edie Greenwood, Connie Threlfall, Betty Brown, Evelyn Threlfall, Margaret Wignall, Jane Parkinson, Kathleen Harrison, Veena Wilson
Middle Row (L–R): Dick Rhodes, Leslie Whittle, Phyllis Worthington, Doris Ashton, Margaret Hodgson, Margaret Whiteside, Grace Buck, Doris Hewitt, Belle Clifton, Elsie Snape, David Fare, George Hawthornthwaite, Mr. Platts
Front Row (L–R): John Whiteside, Jackie Baines, Janie Whittle, Margery Hastwell, Bertha Coulton, Hettie Sudell, Mary Butler, Marie Fisher, Leatrice Hodgson, Clifford Whiteside, Henry Whittle

Courtesy of Mrs. Bertha Loxham formerly Slater (nee Coulton), who also identified the pupils.

experiences during World War I he emphasised the importance and purpose of the conference.

To mark the coronation of King George VI and Queen Elizabeth in May 1937 the pupils were each presented with a medal. And on 17 May 1938 the school was closed in the afternoon when the King and Queen passed through the village. The school log book records that 'the children assembled at 2pm. They were formed up along the school railings and cheered their Majesties as they passed by'.

Mr. Platts, died on 9 February 1939, after being present at school only two days previously. The entry in the school log book described him as ' A good teacher – a good & kind man – a gentleman'. In the same year preliminary approaches were made to the Education Authority for the replacement of the school.

CHAPTER FIVE

The 1944 Air Disaster and New Memorial School

FOLLOWING THE DEATH of Mr. Platts the school managers appointed Frederick Arthur Billington as headmaster. Born in 1906 Mr. Billington was educated at Crewe Secondary School, and from there went to Chester Training College. At Chester he was so successful that he was granted an extra year for study at Liverpool University where he passed the intermediate examination for the B.Sc degree of London University.

He was one of ninety applicants for the post at Freckleton, and at the time of his appointment was headmaster of Cranage C of E School, Holmes Chapel, Cheshire.

In 1943 he initiated the Platts Memorial Fund for helping 'needy grammar school children'. A member of Freckleton Parish Council for nine years from 1951, he was council chairman in 1958. In 1960 he became a Justice of the Peace.

Within two months of his appointment (September 1939) Mr. Billington had to make arrangements for the arrival of children evacuated from Salford due to the outbreak of World War II. When school re-assembled on 11 September 1939 six classes were formed with a combined total (local and evacuees) of two hundred and two pupils. In January 1940 thirty evacuees still remained together with their teacher Miss Hulme.

Freckleton's first experience of the reality of war occurred on 15 September 1940. The following day Mr. Billington recorded in the school log book

> School re-opened. Owing to bombs having been dropped on the village last night at about 11pm demolishing the smithy [located next to the present day Methodist Church], breaking many windows, and causing a number of families to be evacuated from their houses,

many children were absent for part or the whole of the today. 110 yards of net has been received for the protection of children from flying splinters of glass. The air-raid shelters have not yet been commenced

In addition to the problem of overcrowding, the weather too added to the problems of Mr. Billington and his staff. On 31 January 1940 only twenty children arrived at school following a heavy snowfall which, combined with a lack of heating fuel, resulted in the school being closed until 12 February.

As in World War I pupils were encouraged to take an active part in the war effort, and during Warship Week in March 1942 the school group raised £1,420, whilst in the Wings for Victory Week in May 1943 the impressive sum of £5,300 was amassed. At Christmas 1943 the United States Army Air Force, which had been based at Warton since 1942, entertained a total of 178 children over three days at the American Camp.

However, the one single event of World War II that overshadows all others is the disaster that took place on Wednesday 23 August 1944 when an American Liberator bomber crashed onto the school. The school had re-assembled only the previous day following a four week summer holiday. On that day the school register recorded the names of one hundred and seventy six local pupils and fourteen evacuees.

The teaching staff comprised Mr. Billington, Miss Healy, Miss Rawcliffe (later Mrs. Lightfoot), Mrs. Owen, Miss Jennie Hall, a former pupil commencing duties in the Infants Room, and Miss Louisa Hulme from Salford, who was sharing the Infant class with Miss Hall.

The disaster occurred at 10.47am when the Liberator aircraft was reputedly hit by lighting and fell onto the infants department of the school, setting the classroom on fire. This was followed by further violent explosions, and after the crash the 'firemen had difficulty in preventing the flames enveloping the senior school from which children had fled in terror'.[64]

Sir Percy Meadon, director of education for Lancashire, Capt. A. F. Hordern, the chief constable, and Supt. W. T. Hinds were all soon at the scene as were the rescue services. There are many first-hand accounts of the disaster, including those of pupils present at school on the fateful day, and of subsequent rescue attempts,[65] but the words of Mr. Billington himself, written later in the school log book, are perhaps the most poignant of all

> Admitted Sylvia Whybrow and Doris Kempton evacuated from the London Area because of Flying Bombs.
>
> At 10.40am [sic] a thunderstorm was at its height, with torrential rain, and almost complete darkness. As a result, an American Liberator Bomber crashed.

> The windows of the north room were blown in.
>
> Gwen Singleton received extensive burns, and May Hornby and Barbara Cumpsty were suffering from a fractured skull and concussion.
>
> The Infant room was demolished, and enveloped in blazing petrol.
>
> Only seven children and the two teachers were rescued, alive. Thirty four perished immediately. (Both teachers and four children died later.)
>
> The children from the other rooms, all of which were damaged, left the building by means of the door in boys cloakroom under the supervision of their teachers.
>
> Members of the United States Army Air Force and Civil Defence Units were quickly on the scene.
>
> The mornings attendances were cancelled.
>
> Miss Hall died in the Preston Infirmary.

The Ministry of Education was informed immediately of the disaster, and in response a telegram was sent by R. A. Butler, the President of the Board of Education, to the chairman of Lancashire County Council in which he deeply deplored the 'sad tragedy at Freckleton School. My sincerest sympathies go out to all parents affected'.[66]

The inquest was opened on 25 August. In his concluding remarks, three weeks later, the deputy coroner stated that whilst, 'it would be invidious to single out anyone for what they did in their attempts at rescue in this appalling tragedy', he reserved the highest praise for Mr. Billington

> who himself was a member of the Wardens Service in Freckleton and, although his own child was in another part of the School, by his action in an effort to rescue the children and the members of his Staff in the Infants department, he maintained the highest tradition of the Service. There is abundant testimony of the gallant rescue work he performed and no doubt that his action was the means of saving several lives. He sustained considerable injury (by burning) to his hands whilst engaged in this work. Reference too must be made to the great amount of work carried out by him throughout the rest of that day in the interest of the children and their parents[67]

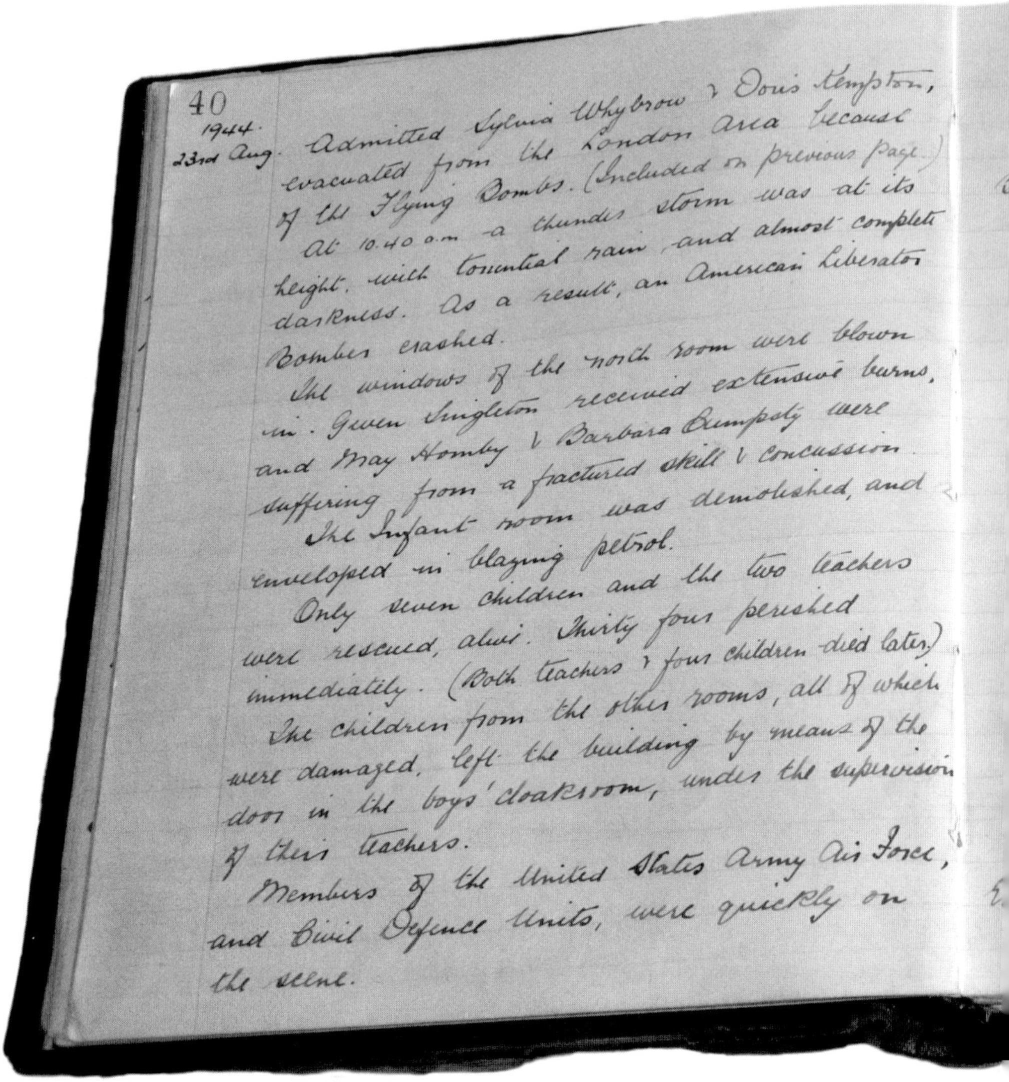

40

1944. 23rd Aug. Admitted Sylvia Whybrow & Doris Kempston, evacuated from the London area because of the Flying Bombs. (Included on previous page.)

At 10.40 a.m. a thunder storm was at its height, with torrential rain, and almost complete darkness. As a result, an American Liberator Bomber crashed.

The windows of the north room were blown in. Gwen Singleton received extensive burns, and May Hornby & Barbara Bumpsty were suffering from a fractured skull & concussion.

The Infant room was demolished, and enveloped in blazing petrol.

Only seven children and the two teachers were rescued, alive. Thirty four perished immediately. (Both teachers & four children died later.)

The children from the other rooms, all of which were damaged, left the building by means of the door in the boys' cloakroom, under the supervision of their teachers.

Members of the United States Army Air Force, and Civil Defence Units, were quickly on the scene.

The funeral service took place on Saturday 26 August when thirty six children, together with their teacher Miss Jennie Hall, were buried in one large communal grave in Holy Trinity churchyard. The seven civilian occupants of the Sad Sack cafe which had stood facing the school, and who had also been killed, were buried in an adjoining grave. The bishop of Blackburn preached the sermon and was assisted at the service by the Rev. J. W. Broadbent (vicar of Freckleton 1930–1950), together with the two village Methodist ministers and the USAAF chaplain.

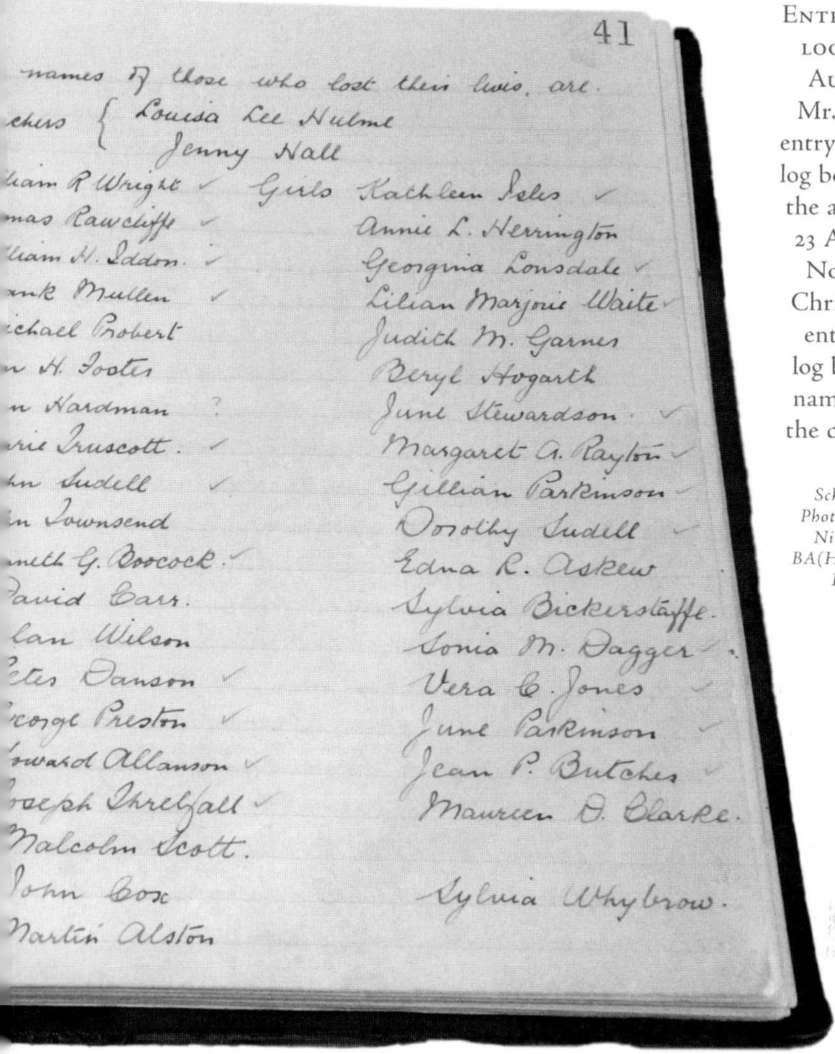
41

names of those who lost their lives, are.

chers { Louisa Lee Hulme
Jenny Hall

liam R Wright ✓ Girls Kathleen Isles ✓
mas Rawcliffe ✓ Annie L. Herrington
lliam H. Iddon ✓ Georgina Lonsdale ✓
ank Mullen ✓ Lilian Marjorie Waite ✓
chael Probert Judith M. Garnes
n H. Foster Beryl Hogarth
n Hardman ? June Stewardson ✓
rie Truscott ✓ Margaret A. Rayton ✓
hn Sudell ✓ Gillian Parkinson ✓
n Townsend Dorothy Sudell ✓
neth G. Boocock ✓ Edna R. Askew
David Carr. Sylvia Bickerstaffe.
lan Wilson Sonia M. Dagger ✓
eter Danson ✓ Vera C. Jones ✓
eorge Preston ✓ June Parkinson ✓
dward Allanson ✓ Jean P. Butcher ✓
oseph Threlfall ✓ Maureen D. Clarke.
Malcolm Scott.
John Cox Sylvia Whybrow.
Martin Alston

Entry in school log book – 23 August 1944
Mr. Billington's entry in the school log book recording the air disaster of 23 August 1944. Note that the Christian names entered in the log book are the names by which the children were known.

School Archives. Photograph by Mrs. Nicole Partridge BA(Hons) of N. Spire Design Ltd.

The American Army Air Force authorities undertook to bear the whole of the expenses. Further internments, including that of Miss. Hulme, took place in the following week, and the final death toll of sixty one comprised thirty eight school-children, two teachers, seven British civilians, four RAF personnel, and ten USAAF airmen, including the three crew members of the Liberator.

The names of the two teachers and thirty-eight schoolchildren who died (the three London evacuees are noted with an asterisk) were

Miss Jennie Hall
Miss Louisa L. Hulme

Howard Allanson
Martin P. Alston *
Edna Rae Askew
Sylvia Bickerstaffe
Kenneth G. Boocock
Jean Butcher
David Carr
Maureen D. Clarke
John Cox *
Sonia M. Dagger
Peter Danson
John H. Foster
Judith M. Garner
John Hardman
Annie L. Herrington
Beryl Hogarth
William H. Iddon
Elizabeth M. K. Isles
Vera C. Jones
Georgina Lonsdale
Thomas F. Mullen
Gillian Parkinson
June Parkinson
George Preston
Michael Probert
Thomas Rawcliffe
Alice M. Rayton
Malcolm Scott
June Stewartson
Dorothy Sudell
John Sudell
Joseph Threlfall
John Townsend
Barrie B. Truscott
Lilian M. Waite
Alice S. Whybrow *
Alan Wilson
Richard W. Wright

The three survivors from the infant's class were George Carey, David Madden, and Ruby Whittle.

On 28 August Mr. S. Lamplugh, the H.M. Inspector responsible for Freckleton, prepared a very detailed report on the disaster for the Ministry of Education.[68] He noted 'that the death roll was not greater through panic is no doubt due to the courage, promptitude and presence of mind of the Headmaster, Mr. F. A. Billington, and the other members of his Staff, Mrs. F. M. Owen, Miss H. Healy and Miss J. E. Rawcliffe'.

Mr. Lamplugh also noted that

> The school premises are in such a condition that it will be impossible to use them for some time. The infant room has completely gone and three of the four remaining rooms have been badly damaged, there are big cracks in the walls and the window frames have been burnt. The remaining room has suffered least but the windows are damaged and there may also be other defects not yet discovered. What seems remarkable is that any of the building should have been left.

His concluding remarks, and no doubt mindful of the events of 1925, attempted to anticipate the future of education in Freckleton

> The future of the school, however, will have to be carefully considered.
>
> The present premises are situated on a very busy thoroughfare, the school is old, has no free space and is awkwardly planned; further it is very likely that to put it into a sound condition again will be a costly job.
>
> It is not unlikely that there will be a demand for a new Council School in the village – there is a very strong Nonconformist [sic] element here and some years ago there was this same demand which may now be renewed very vigorously. If so, and if the Church School Managers feel themselves unable to rebuild the school and agree to give it up – I have no warrant for thinking that they may do so – I imagine that an entirely new school away from the present premises and from the busy main road would be the better thing.
>
> This, however, is a matter for the future; for the present some temporary arrangement will be necessary and the Ministry can rest assured that this problem is being tackled forthwith.

In the days immediately following the disaster every effort was indeed made to provide temporary accommodation until the school could be repaired and reopened. On 30 August Sir Percy Meadon paid a second visit to Freckleton, and by 1 September Mr Billington was able to report that all surviving teachers 'were present'. The following day he wrote that 'The idea of temporary accommodation on the American Camp has been abandoned', but on 4 September he was able to record that equipment had been 'transferred to Kirkham Road Methodist [Sunday] School [room]'.

The school re-opened in the Kirkham Road schoolroom on 5 September when one hundred and four pupils, out of a possible one hundred and forty three, were present. But the horror of the disaster was clearly evident when on 6 September Mr. Billington wrote 'Continuous rain reduced the attendance'.

On the same day (6 September) the request 'from the electors' for a council school, which, as we have seen, had been anticipated by Mr. Lamplugh in his report of 28 August, was received by Coun. Matthew Armstrong, chairman of Freckleton Parish Council. As a result of the request a special meeting of the ratepayers was called, to be held on 18 September.[69]

The request for a council school was almost certainly in response to a decision taken by Holy Trinity parochial church council on 29 August to make two appeals – a local one for a monument in the churchyard, and a general one for funds towards the building of a new church school.

An alternative view, however, was taken by Coun. Matthew Armstrong who was also a school manager. In an interview with the *Lancashire Daily Post* he considered that 'the parish council is the proper body, as elected representatives, to make an appeal for a village memorial'. He added that he did 'not consider Freckleton's memorial should take the form of a new church school'. In his view 'a village hall for all the people would be more suitable'.[70]

A similar view was expressed by Coun. Walter Rawsthorne who represented Freckleton on Fylde Rural District Council. Coun. Rawsthorne was recorded as saying, though on what evidence he based his statement is unclear, that 'Freckleton would like to see the church school restored as a Sunday school, but the form of the village memorial should be decided by the people as a whole'.[71]

Within two days (9 September) of these comments appearing in the local press Rev. Broadbent, in his capacity as chairman of the school managers, sent a circular letter to every home in the village outlining his vision for the future of education in the village

> The recent 'Plane Crash during a violent storm, which wrecked the Infant School in this parish and caused the death of the two teachers and 38 infant scholars, has evoked widespread sympathy throughout the country. In spite of these sad happenings the world must go on, and the Education of future generations is of paramount importance. Freckleton Parish School has been in existence for over 100 years and has turned out many good citizens who have brought credit to their teachers and the parish. The Infant Department has been totally destroyed, and the remainder of the School premises badly damaged. It has been decided to make such temporary repairs as may be possible and, with the kind assistance of our Methodist friends, who have loaned their schoolroom, to carry on School as best we can until a new building can be provided.
>
> The object of this letter is to say that the Church authorities have decided to build a "Memorial School" on a new and admirable site in the centre of the village directly circumstances permit. The cost of the proposed building will not be less than £15,000. The Bishop of the Diocese authorizes me to say that he strongly supports the scheme as the most practical and permanent form of memorial. I desire to point out that the names of all who perished in this disaster will be recorded – the members of the crew of the 'plane

and also those killed in the "Snack Bar", and this proposal is warmly approved by all concerned.

Rev. Broadbent concluded his letter by saying that a subscription list was now open and that accounts had been opened at the 'District and Midland Banks in Freckleton'.

On the 11 September Sir Percy Meadon informed Mr. Lamplugh that, at the request of the school managers, he had arranged for the county architect to arrange for the necessary repairs to be carried out on 'a cost plus basis'. He added that the 'representatives of the Air Ministry have agreed to the principle of reinstating the School with the exception of the Infants' classroom'. A month later the Ministry of Education confirmed that 'the execution of repairs estimated to cost £750 approximately' had been approved.[72]

The previously mentioned special meeting of the ratepayers was held on 18 September. The meeting was held on the petition of six electors, though, as we shall see, the petition was subsequently signed by three hundred and twenty five ratepayers. The chief proponent for a council school was Mr. W. E. Durant, the village chemist, who stated his case, principally, on financial grounds. This argument was countered by Rev. Broadbent. Differing views were expressed by various speakers, including appeals that 'religious differences should be sunk in the general educational welfare of the children'.[73]

Mr. Robert Newton Wignall, who later provided the land for the new school, pleaded that it was not an opportune time for consideration of a council school. He added that 'it was not the time to make an attack on religious education. The church school and its pupils had suffered through no fault of their own. It was almost like stabbing them in the back. A new church school would be built on a new site'.[74]

Mr. Tom Banks suggested that the whole question should be left to the Lancashire Education Committee, and at the end of the meeting it was decided not to vote on a proposal that the time was opportune to approach Lancashire Education Committee with a view to providing a council school in the parish.[75]

However, as we shall see, it does appear that the petition for a council school was forwarded to the Lancashire Education Committee, and as a result all future discussions, whether at Lancashire Education Committee or at the Ministry of Education, could not, and indeed did not, ignore the opinion of a considerable number of the village population.

On 18 October Sir Percy Meadon wrote to the Ministry of Education enclosing a memorandum that had been adopted by Lancashire Education Committee as a basis 'on which a scheme of Divisional Administration for the County may be considered and formulated'. He also advised the ministry that Canon (later Archdeacon) Lambert, a member of the Lancashire Education

Committee and of the Blackburn Diocesan Council for Religious Education, had requested a meeting with officials at the Ministry of Education 'to clear up several points ... about the position of Church of England Schools under the new Education Act'.[76]

In a letter dated 24 October Canon Lambert summarised the points he wished to raise

> (1) Under the new Education Act, the existing site at Freckleton School will almost certainly be regarded as being too restricted to permit of the necessary alterations and improvements. Another site will have to be secured and this would be regarded as a transferred site and, therefore, under the terms of the new Act, the Lancashire Education Authority would be responsible for its purchase. But the destruction of the Infants Department has made it necessary to provide new accommodation for Infants as early as possible. Such accommodation cannot be provided on the existing site. It would be foolish to make the attempt in view of the probability of the existing School being transferred to another site.
>
> Therefore, a new site should be obtained now and it would be wise to secure a site which would provide for a junior Mixed School as well as an Infant School. But if a site is secured now, the cost presumably will fall upon the Managers. It is rather hard that the Managers should be called upon to face this expense now through circumstances over which they had no control, when very shortly, in all probability, the expense would fall upon the L.E.A. Is there any way of getting over this difficulty?
>
> (2) Will the Ministry agree to the building of a new Infant Department or School with the possibility of a Nursery Class immediately, it being clearly understood that such Department or School is part of a scheme for the erection of a Junior Mixed School as an Aided School under the new Act?
>
> (3) If an Infant School is built, can it be regarded as Aided School and will the 50% grant be available?

The questions raised by Canon Lambert resulted in the Ministry of Education carrying out a very through review of the situation at Freckleton, in particular as to whether any new school should be a continuity of the Church school, or an undenominational (council) school.

The situation was also reviewed by Mr. Lamplugh who pointed out that

RETURN TO SCHOOL
In the weeks immediately following the air disaster classes were held at the Wesleyan Methodist Sunday schoolroom. Trinity School re-opened on 30 October 1944 when the four infants present were accommodated with Standard 1. Mrs. Owen, who had been in another classroom on the day of the disaster, is seen guiding the returning children towards the school.
Courtesy of David Kirby.

'it should be made perfectly clear at the outset that there was no Infants Department at the school. It was and is an "all-age" school which had two infants' classes'. He also observed that due to the air disaster there were few children in the 4+ and 5+ age groups, and that this age gap would 'be evident throughout the school for some years'. This element combined with the fact that all of the 14+ age group would leave by 1 August 1945 would mean that 'on numbers therefore the school has plenty of room'.[77]

Although this now sounds to be have been a somewhat dispassionate assessment it should be remembered that by 1944 more than five thousand schools had been destroyed or damaged by enemy action during World War II. And, as we have seen, there was also the contentious local matter of whether to build a Church or undenominational school.

With regard to whether the L.E.A would object to making temporary provision for additional classrooms Mr. Lamplugh advised the Ministry of Education that Sir Percy Meadon considered that 'any such step would not be politic'. He continued by pointing out that the 'Nonconformists' [sic] had petitioned Lancashire County Council to build a Council School to replace the present C of E School. The petition had been signed by three hundred and twenty five ratepayers, which, in the opinion of Mr. Lamplugh was a 'considerable number in this smallish place'. However, he added that the L.E.A., 'by the way, have as yet merely noted the receipt of this petition'.[78]

Mr Lamplugh concluded by stating that Sir Percy Meadon was concerned that any action on the part of the L.E.A. which appeared to favour 'the Church party' would 'lead to a storm'. Mr. Lamplugh, therefore, suggested that the school managers 'would be well advised to hold their hand at the moment so far as any building is concerned & to hire temporary accommodation for an infant class when provision for such becomes necessary'.[79]

By 30 October Mr. Billington was able to record that 'Re-opened school in the premises damaged by the plane on 23rd August. There being no class room for the 4 infants present [in the 4+ age group], they were accommodated in room 4 together with Standard I.' And on 2 November he noted that the workmen had completed the fencing, the bicycle shed, and the interior decoration of the school.

Three weeks later, on 17 November, the meeting between Sir Percy Meadon, Canon Lambert, and officials at the Ministry of Education took place. The situation at Freckleton was reviewed, and it was agreed that, as far as the actual premises and accommodation went, the position was satisfactory. Indeed, it was considered that the buildings as restored were better than they had ever been and the accommodation was adequate for the number of children currently on the register, and for the estimated requirements of the school in the immediate future.

The discussion then turned to the line to be taken by the Church to ensure the future of the school as a denominational one, in opposition to those who were pressing 'their claims for a council school'.[80] In an internal Ministry of Education memo, two days previously, Mr. Burrows, a senior official at the Ministry, had noted that during the parliamentary debate great emphasis had been laid on section 76 of the 1944 Education Act which set out that if there was a strong enough local demand for a council school, it may be necessary to contemplate issuing notices and providing such a school.

If, however, the L.E.A. were to decide to transfer the school, and if the Minister, approved the proposal under the Local Education Order, it would be up to the school managers to decide whether they applied for the school to be an aided [church] school, or whether they wished it to be a controlled [council]school. If the managers decided the school should be an aided school, to be transferred to new premises on a new site, it would be for the L.E.A. to provide the site, and they would have compulsory purchase for that purpose. If the new school was a controlled school the full financial responsibility would in future fall upon the L.E.A.

Sir Percy Meadon and Canon Lambert initially urged that the Church should take immediate action to bring out a definite building proposal. However, Mr. Burrows pointed out that as there was an extreme shortage of building labour it was unlikely that the project proposed could 'plead sufficient urgency to merit an allocation of labour'.[81]

In view of these considerations Sir Percy Meadon proposed a compromise. He suggested that the Church, while taking no further action as regards the purchase of the site in question, could, nevertheless, launch an immediate appeal for money for the future school putting forward definite proposals for the new building, supplemented perhaps by a plan which his architects could help Canon Lambert produce. This line of action would have the advantage of making the Church's policy clear but not involving it in the expense of buying the site.

Sir Percy Meadon did not consider there was any danger of the Church losing the land it coveted by delaying the purchase since there was unlikely to be much building development in Freckleton, but, even if this improbable contingency did occur, there was plenty more suitable land.

In response Mr. Burrows pointed out that all such risk could be avoided by reserving the land for educational purposes with the Town Planning Authority. He added that no guarantee could, of course, be given that the school to be erected would be a Church school, and subsequently annotated the minutes of the meeting with the comment 'we cannot ignore the views of three hundred and twenty five ratepayers in a little place like this'.[82] However, it was not until 1953 that any decision was made, and approval was given finally in favour of a new Church school.

Throughout 1945 and 1946 school-life continued in accordance with the educational requirements of the day. On 24 May 1947 the dedication and unveiling of the 10 ft high Gothic cross erected on the communal grave of the victims of the air disaster took place. The cross was unveiled by Coun. J. S. Barlow who had lost two grandchildren in the disaster. The dedication was carried out by bishop Askwith of Blackburn, and the cost of nearly £1,100 was subscribed by the families of the bereaved and their friends.

By early 1947 Mr. Billington and his staff were faced with the additional task of implementing the requirements of the 1944 Education Act. The Act provided free secondary education for all pupils, and also raised the school leaving age to fifteen. It also introduced the examination known as the "11

Rebuilt School
Following the 1944 air disaster the Air Ministry agreed to 're-instating the school with the exception of the infants classroom'. The infants transferred to the New Memorial School in 1955 but the junior classes continued to be taught at the "old" (Trinity) school until 1970, when Phase III of the New Memorial School opened. Trinity School was demolished in 1974: properties on Trinity Close now occupy the site.
Courtesy of Lancashire Evening Post.

plus" with the intended aim of providing equal opportunities for children of all backgrounds to continue their education at grammar, secondary modern, or technical school.

Due to the lack of secondary educational establishments in the area most pupils, other than those who had passed their "scholarship" for Kirkham Grammar School; King Edward VII School, Lytham; Queen Mary School, Lytham; or Park School for Girls, Preston, remained at the school.

To provide some extra curricular activity various events were organised. On 11 September 1947 the 'top class' visited Ravald Farm in three groups, and a fortnight later five girls visited Bush Farm to study cheese making. And on 29

November 1948 thirty pupils were taken to Freckleton College, Naze Lane, to see 'the Local Survey Exhibition'.

In April 1949, due to the ever increasing number of pupils, 'an additional class was formed and taken by Miss Hayward at the Preston Old Road Primitive Methodist Schoolroom'. On 22 July the same year, when the school closed for the summer holiday, thirteen children in the fourteen plus age group left as 'arrangements have been made for them to attend the Lytham St Anne's Technical School after the holiday'. In September 1951 most of those in the fourteen plus age group were transferred to classes held at Ansdell Institute.

Prior to attending their final year at Ansdell Institute a small numbers of pupils were given the opportunity, by Lancashire Education Authority, to attend boarding school. Several boys attended Horsley Green Camp School, High Wycombe, where they slept in dormitories. Discipline was strict and they had to up at 7am every morning and keep their personal belongings neat and tidy. The curriculum included English, Arithmetic, Science, Metalwork,

MEMORIAL TO THE VICTIMS OF THE 1944 AIR DISASTER
The memorial to the victims of the 1944 air disaster was unveiled on 24 May 1947 by Coun. J. S. Barlow who had lost two grandchildren in the disaster. The total death toll was sixty one, including thirty eight children and two teachers who had been present in the infants classroom.
Photograph by Mrs. Sue Scholz.

Miss Hilda Healy and Class of 1949
Back Row (L–R): Peter Holliday, David Turner, Jim Gibson, Harry Whiteside, Robert Hornby, Alan Watkinson, Peter Sobey
Fourth Row (L–R): Miss Healy, Terry Unsworth, Marlene Christopher, Elaine Beck, Barbara Wignall, Jane Lonsdale, Elizabeth Williamson, Elizabeth Wade, Geoff Worthington
Third Row (L–R): Marie Norwood, Irene McCarthy, Kathleen Bannister, Catherine Sudell, Rhona Danson, Ann Norwood, Avril Gardner, Thelma Turner
Second (L–R): Greta Eastham, Ann Fisher, Esther Midgley, Sylvia Birch, Jenny Joule, Ruth Waite, Margaret Fox, Susan Fail
Front Row (L–R): Not known, Adrian Norcross, John Rayton, Geoffrey Snape, Dick Crane, Jimmy Waite, Not known, Sam Clitheroe, Tony Danson, Derek Rawstrone (behind Tony Danson)
Miss Healy was present in another classroom on the day of the 1944 air disaster. She attended the memorial service to mark the 60th anniversary of the disaster (2004) shortly before her death aged 85.

School Archives. Pupils identified by Mrs. Jenny Payne (nee Joule), Alan Watkinson, Harry Whiteside, and Mrs. Barbara Welbourne (nee Wignall).

Mrs. Joan Lightfoot (nee Rawcliffe) and Class of 1950
Back Row (L–R): Henry Steele, Tony Danson, Alan Watkinson, Berrick Wilson, Gordon Porter, George Carey, Bobbie Crankshaw, Stuart Gibson, Peter Holliday, Mrs. Lightfoot
Third Row (L–R): Ruby Whittle, Jane Lonsdale, Joan Latham, Jean McCarthy, June Midgley, Kathleen Clitheroe, Lorna Roocroft, Edna Salisbury, Rosemary Williamson, Stella Bowling, Margaret Kirby, David Turner
Second Row (L–R): John Hull, Greta Eastham, Ann Norwood, Jenny Joule, Maureen Coates, Doreen Whittle, Grace Williamson, Sylvia Birch, Jean Templeton, Elaine Beck, John Crane
Front Row (L–R): Maureen Almond, Peter Sobey, Jack Woods, Angie Ball

School Archives. Pupils identified by Mrs. Ruby Currell (nee Whittle).

Frederick Arthur Billington (headmaster) and Class of 1950
Back Row (L–R): Benny Walker, Ronnie McLaughlin, Colin Clifton, Douglas Truscott, Edward Dawson, Tom Fare, John Fisher, Ronnie Woods, Cuthbert Fare, Billy Butcher, Jack Disley, Mr. Billington
Third Row (L–R): Roy Kiddle, Una Mullen, Barbara Proctor, Eileen Butler, Shirley Cowburn, Marlene Singleton, Irene Rayton, Greta Danson, Robert Bamber, Harry Allanson
Second Row (L–R): Not known, Mildred Kilburn, Lilian Salthouse, Freda Walsh, Kathleen Waite, Joan Singleton, Jane Bamber, Renee Barlow, Margaret Boocock, Margaret Iddon, Harold Banks
Front Row (L–R): Peggy Rawcliffe, Jean Eastham

School Archives. Pupils identified by Cuthbert Fare, and Mrs. Jean Hardy (nee Eastham).

School Concert c1950/1

Throughout the late 1940s and 1950s various events were organised in order to raise funds for the New Memorial School. This particular concert was held at the "old" (Trinity) School.

Back Row (L–R): Irene Iddon, Eileen Preston, Doreen Whiteside, Peggy Rawcliffe, Betty Iddon

Middle Row (L–R): Ruby Whittle, Joan Latham, Edna Salisbury, Eric Bickerstaffe, Gordon Hetherington, Mark Rossall, Gordon Porter, David Turner, Jean McCarthy, Audrey Birch, Sylvia Birch, Greta Eastham, Maureen Coates, Elaine Beck, Dorothy Barlow

Front Row (L–R): Karen Muncaster, Irene McCarthy, Sandra Whitworth, Marlene Christopher, Tony Beck, Maureen Carey, Ruth Helm, Jane Lonsdale, Thelma Turner, Reg McCarthy, Sandra Muncaster, Tommy Greenwood, Eileen Henvey, Angela Lonsdale

Courtesy of Mrs. Maureen Shakeshaft (nee Coates), who also identified the pupils.

Laying of foundation stone for New Memorial School
On 25 September 1954 the foundation stone of the New Memorial School was laid in memory of those who died in the 1944 air disaster by the Rev. J .W. Broadbent (vicar of Freckleton 1930-1950). The stone was blessed by the Rt. Rev. Dr. Benjamin Pollard (suffragan bishop of Lancaster).
(Left / Centre) Canon H. G. Potter (vicar of St Thomas', St Anne's, and rural dean), Rev. G. O. Clayton ?, Mr. A. Leach (diocesan architect), Rt. Rev. Dr. Pollard
Right (L–R) Mr. T. Joyce (contractor), Rev. Broadbent, Rev. H. C. Pope (vicar of Freckleton 1950-1959), Lieut-Col G. M. Rogers (USAF, Burtonwood)
Courtesy of Lytham St Annes Express.

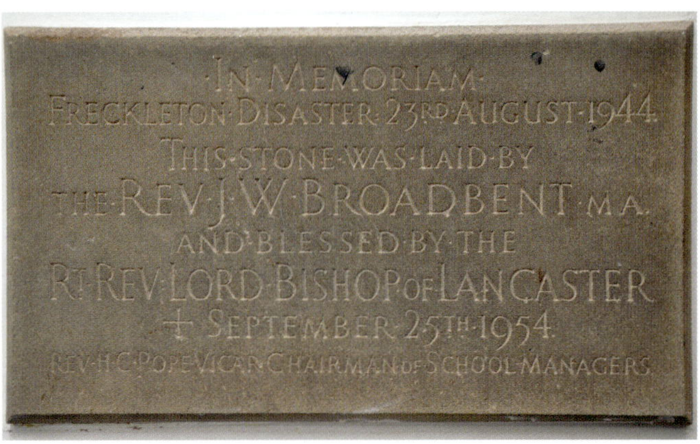

Foundation stone – New Memorial School
The foundation stone of the New Memorial School located just inside the entrance to the school.
Photograph by Mrs. Nicola Partridge BA(Hons) of N. Spire Design Ltd.

and Woodwork.[83] Several girls attended Whalley Girls School, known as Whiteacres, where they too slept in dormitories. Extra curriculum activities included dancing, needlework, and outdoor pursuits.[84]

Whilst it was inevitable that local events dominated school life the pupils were always made aware of significant national events. In 1951 a visit was organised to the "Festival of Britain" in London, which also included visits to other sites including Westminster Abbey. Accommodation was in bunk beds at Clapham Common underground shelters that had been used as air-raid shelters during World War II.[85]

On 6 February 1952 the 'children stood in silence' when the BBC announced the death King George VI. And from 22 May to 8 June 1953 the school was closed for Whitsuntide 'and for the Coronation of Her Majesty Queen Elizabeth II'. On 2 July 1953 forty six seniors and juniors, accompanied by Mr. Billington and three other members of staff, left Freckleton for a two day holiday to London where they again visited Westminster Abbey, and also St Pauls' Cathedral, the Tower of London, and Regent's Park Zoo. Overnight accommodation, on this occasion, was at a camp school at Chigwell.

On 7 September the same year (1953) the Rev. Herbert Pope (vicar of Freckleton 1950–1959), together with Mr. Billington, attended a meeting at the Ministry of Education, when, according to the entry in the school log book 'Important proposals were made'.

The "important proposals" were an advance notice that Lancashire Education Authority were about to recommend to the county council the purchase of reserved land for a new school at a site in School Lane (which, as we have seen, was so named after the eighteenth century Quaker school). The recommendation was put forward on 16 November 1953 and approved.

The reserved land, which had been offered by Robert Newton Wignall, contained an area of approximately three and a half acres, and was freehold and free from chief rent. The purchase price was agreed at £525 plus £364 for the apportioned development value.[86]

By 1954 events were moving rapidly. On 3 May that year 'all scholars over 11 on 1st September' were transferred to the St Anne's Senior School (Ansdell Institute) 'in order that children aged 5+ may be admitted'. On 14 June, when the school re-opened after the Whitsun holiday, '20 children [were] transferred to the [RAF] Kirkham Camp School'.

In the same year work began on Phase 1 of the new buildings in School Lane, with the provision of three infant classrooms. It was decided that the name of the school should be the Freckleton New Memorial School (usually referred to as the "new" school), and on Saturday 25 September 1954 the foundation stone was laid by Rev. Broadbent, the former vicar. The stone was blessed by bishop Pollard of Lancaster who said that 'We are here to lay a foundation stone and

Miss Helen Hayward and Class of 1953
Back Row (L–R): June Crossley, John Whiteside, Janet Snape, Tommy Garlick, David Kirby, John Baxendale, Eveline Hayes, Rodney Gregson, Stanley Parkinson, Jackie Whittle, Janet Carter, Miss Hayward
Third Row (L–R): Harry Hall, David Redmond, Reggie Hardman, Peter Bamber, Rowan Bowling, Arnold Sandford, Peter Rawstrone, Bill Henvey, Richard Rayton, Not known
Second Row (L–R): Jennifer Rogers ?, Not known, Carole Bartlett, Judy Garlick, Christine Rhodes, Jennifer Hole, Celia Dickinson, Maureen Throp, Pamela Cliffe, Kathleen Winwood, Irene McDowell
Front Row (L–R): Michael Worthington, John Rossall, Trevor Bailey, Craig Morris, John Holliday, Edwin Rawstrone ?, Alan Gregson

Courtesy of David Kirby. Pupils identified by David Kirby, and Mrs. Kathleen Nuttall (nee Winwood).

FOOTBALL TEAM 1953/4

In the 1953/4 season the school football team beat Heyhouses School 2-0 in the final of inter-school Rotary Cup trophy at Seafield Road, Lytham.

Back Row (L–R): Barry Helm, Steven Baxendale, Adrian Ley, Jimmy Marshall, Mark Rossall, Phillip Kay

Front Row (L–R): Peter Norcross, Trevor Fiddler, Bert Templeton, Reg McCarthy, David Banks

Graham Doughty, the goalkeeper, was not present when the photograph was taken. Bert Templeton was captain. Phillip Kay was the reserve. The scorers were Templeton and Baxendale.

Courtesy of Steven Baxendale, who also provided the names and information.

Class of 1954
Back Row (L–R): David Crane, Alan Preston, Bert Templeton, Stuart Smith, Michael Parkinson, Grenville Parker, Len Isles, Terry Guest, Charles Whittle, Geoff Anyon, Barry Proctor, Peter ?, Terry Unsworth
Third Row (L–R): Kathleen Ormrod, Heather Slatcher, Rita Woods, Ann Threlfall, Jenny Fare, Christine Bannister, Thelma Turner, Christine Hart, Caroline ?, Shirley Whittle, Elizabeth Wade, Doreen Throp, Pamela Davies
Second Row (L–R): Valerie Cartmell, Maureen Scholz, Muriel Bramley, Grace West, Marlene Midgley, Pat Ball, Sandra Whitworth, Elizabeth Mason, Dorothy Barlow, Maureen Sidebotham, Joan Brown, Jean Henvey, Wendy Richmond
Front Row (L–R): Winnie Wilson, Alan Wright, Steven Baxendale, Barry Helm, Michael Richardson, Peter Allen, Reg McCarthy, Jim Iddon, Peter Norcross, Carol Porter

School Archives. Pupils identified by Mrs. Ann Kay (nee Threlfall).

Class of 1954

Back Row (L–R): Tommy Greenwood, Michael McDowell, Keith Sidebotham, Terry Scholz, Gordon Hetherington, Butch Molyneux, Trevor Fiddler, Mark Rossall, Arthur Baxendale, Tony Beck, Philip Kay, David Banks, John Snape

Third Row (L–R): Eric Hassall, Mark Heald, Terry Carter, Jimmy Marshall, Arthur Gibson, Michael Hankinson, Not known, Adrian Ley, John Gregson, Roger Fail, Eric Bickerstaffe, Peter Harwood, Graham Doughty

Second Row (L–R): Pat Hazelgrove, Kathleen Molyneux, Carol Ball, Linda Smith, Ann Coppings, Not known, Maureen Dickinson, Gladys Threlfall, Linda Stewartson, Jean Helm, Ruth Waite

Front Row (L–R): Drena Anyon, Gloria Wilkinson, Susan Billington, Angela Lonsdale, Sheila Barlow, June Kirby, Not known, Joyce Rayton, Celia Dickinson ?

School Archives. Pupils identified by Mrs. Drena Crone (nee Anyon), Mark Rossall, and Mrs. Joyce Shaw (nee Rayton).

Left Class of 1954

Back Row (L–R): Eric Coates, Gerald Wright, Leslie Parkinson, David Crossley, Jim Henvey, Jim and John Snape, Gordon Butcher, Roger Waite, David Smith, Not known

Third Row (L–R): Alvar Unsworth, Walter Norcross, Tony Dagger, Eric Cartmell Stanley Cartmell, David Parkinson, Peter Norcross, Ken Isles, John Rawcliffe, Not known, Jack Parkinson

Second Row (L–R): Kathleen Boocock, Not known, Rita English, Mary Sudell, Sandra Muncaster, Lesley Truscott, Vivien ?, Jennifer Hall, Not known, Karen Muncaster, Janice Bartlett

Front Row (L–R): Roger Parkinson, Michael Hacking, Linda Rhodes, Betty Danson, Joyce English, Joan Iddon, Maureen Gregson, Bobby Horrocks, David Eastham

School Archives. Pupils identified by Mrs. Carole Bell (nee Bartlett), Mrs. Karen Pye (nee Muncaster), Mark Rossall and Mrs. Mary Rossall (nee Sudell), and Mrs. Jennifer Thompson (nee Hall).

Mrs. Margaret Salthouse (nee Kirby) and Class of 1956
Back Row (L–R): Roger Throp, Greg Fiddler, Michael Parkinson, Gary McLaughlin, Michael Woods, Billy Stewartson, Norman Hassall, Michael Appleton, Roger White, Mrs. Salthouse
Third Row (L–R): Not known, Leonard Kemery, Steven Hunter, Peter Hardman, David Whiteside, David Fisher, Matthew Tellum, Michael Haglow, Frank Kemery, Barry Sidebotham
Second Row (L–R): Not known, Joyce Buck, Stephanie Dagger, Eileen Willacy, Dorothy Hall, Helen Rhodes, Marion Waite, Janet Lancaster, Linda Leeming
Front Row (L–R): David Cartmell, Brenda Cartmell, Graham Whittle, Jennifer Keyes, Malcolm Montgomery
Courtesy of David Fisher, who also identified the pupils.

Mrs. F. Margery Owen and Class of 1956
Back Row (L–R): Alan McCarthy, Kenneth Hayes, Philip Brown, Stephen Throp, Alan Hall, David Nicholls, Peter Bartlett, Mrs. Owen
Third Row (L–R): Peter Scholz, Peter Lawler, Not known, Graham Cartmell, Peter Nunn, Billy Hole, Ian Robinson, Jack Finch
Second Row (L–R): Diane Wright, Marilyn Cavan, Anne Garlick, Margaret Sandford, Dorothy Seddon, Elsie Sandford, Judy Parkinson, Margaret Rigby, Sylvia Dickinson
Front Row (L–R): Pauline Kay, Sheena Rogers, Eileen Henvey, Judy Bromby, Diane Bailey, Sandra Marshall, Mary McDowell, Linda Holliday

Courtesy of David Kirby, who also identified the pupils.

Frederick Arthur Billington and teaching staff 1956
Frederick Arthur Billington was headmaster from 1939 to 1958. At the inquest following the 1944 air disaster the coroner praised 'the gallant rescue work he performed' adding that 'no doubt his action was the means of saving several lives'.
Harry Rothwell subsequently became headmaster of Warton Church of England School.
Standing: Harry Rothwell.
Seated (L–R): Miss Jean Crossley, Frederick Arthur Billington, Mrs. F. Margery Owen
School Archives.

to bless the building of this school, which will always be a living memorial – not something that is just put up and, as is often the case, so easily forgotten'.[87]

By May 1955 the H.M. Inspector was able to report that 'the first three classrooms are almost ready for completion and occupation'. The cost was £10,107 19s. 10d., of which the managers' share was £4236 12s. 10d. The inspector added that 'there are 200 children of 5 to 11 years attending the school, they are taught in six classes'. Included in the subjects for the infants were 'Reading, Writing, and Numbers, P.E., Music & Painting'. For the juniors subjects included 'Diaries, History, Geography, Nature Study, Needlework & Crafts, Music, Art, and P.E.'.

The New Memorial School opened on 1 September 1955. The fact that the school was now functioning on two sites cannot have been easy for Mr. Billington and his staff. It must, therefore, have been encouraging for them when, on 20 February 1958, the managers met and signed the contract for an assembly hall, kitchen, and staff room to be added to the New Memorial School. These additions, known as Phase II, were officially opened on 22 April 1959, by vicar Pope. The cost was £12,580 5s. 1d., of which the manager's share was £2303 10s. 9d. A significant amount of the latter money was raised through regular fund-raising events such as the annual "Sale of Work" which, for example, on 6 November 1959 raised £450.

Although, throughout the 1960s, the focus was very much on the New Memorial School the original Trinity School (by now usually referred to as the "old" school) also had to be maintained, and in September 1961 it was completely rewired with new electrical fittings.

By the 1960s the health of the children was greatly improved when compared with that of their great grandparents a century earlier. Nevertheless there were still the inevitable regular outbreaks of various illnesses as on 11 January 1962 when 'following the fog, snow, frost, and gales' many children were absent 'with colds & influenza & chicken pox'. Other diseases were however slowly being eradicated thanks to advances in medical science, and on 1 February 1966 'many children [were] given the first oral anti polio vaccine'.

Although some of the problems of an overcrowded school had been addressed by the early 1960s, it was not until 1965 that there was another primary school in the village. In that year Strike Lane County Primary School was built as a replacement for Kirkham RAF County Primary School. The school was designed in three phases between 1965 and 1970, and with its formal opening the "undenominational school", first requested over forty years earlier, was finally built. Even so, when the combined Trinity / New Memorial School opened for a new term on 30 August 1966, there were still two hundred and thirty six pupils on the school roll.

Two years later, on 16 July 1968, and after twenty nine years of committed and dedicated service to the school, Frederick Billington resigned as headmaster. His twenty nine years service almost equaled that of James Bramwell half a century earlier. Mr. Billington continued to reside in the village at Cranford, Preston Old Road, until his death on 28 April 1975.

UNVEILING OF PLAQUE IN MEMORY OF THE TEACHERS AND PUPILS WHO DIED IN THE 1944 AIR DISASTER

A plaque in memory of the teachers and pupils who died in the 1944 air disaster was unveiled at the present school on 1 November 1963 by the Ven. C. H. Lambert (centre) (vicar of Lytham and archdeacon of Lancaster). On the left is Rev. N. S. Saul (vicar of Freckleton 1959–1966), and on the right F. A. Billington (headmaster). Archdeacon Lambert had an influential role in ensuring the New Memorial School was built.

Courtesy of Lytham St Annes Express.

CHAPTER SIX

Into the modern era

FREDERICK BILLINGTON WAS SUCCEEDED as headmaster by George Eric Ray. Mr Ray was born in 1924 in Staffordshire and, as a Sub Lieutenant R.N.V.R., served in Combined Operations during World War II. His teaching training was at Chester Diocesan Training College, and one of his earliest appointments was as deputy headmaster at St Peter's C of E School, Formby. At the time of his appointment to Freckleton he was headmaster at Wesham C of E School.

At various times during his career he was a member of the Diocesan Schools Committee, a member of the National Schools Council (Religious Education Committee), and president and secretary of the Fylde Association of the National Union of Teachers. He introduced the school uniform of blue and brown and the school badge and motto "In fide scientia consistat" (Let knowledge be grounded in faith). He also served as a sidesman at Holy Trinity Church, and as secretary of the parochial church council.

Mr. Ray took up his appointment on 27 August 1968. He inherited a school with two departments, one in the "old" school in four junior classes, and one in the "new" school in three infant classes. They were working independently even to marking the registers differently.[88]

Within a month of his appointment Mr. Ray had organised a parents evening that was attended by one hundred and twenty people. At the event he gave a talk entitled "Primary Schools", after which it was unanimously agreed to form "An Association of Parents, Teachers & Friends of Freckleton C of E School". A committee of twelve under the chairmanship of Mr. Ray was elected. Other new innovations introduced by Mr. Ray included the post of a school clerk, a post for which there were no less than twelve applicants. About this time the name of the school was changed to Freckleton Church of England Primary School.

School Badge
Shortly after his appointment as headteacher in 1968 Mr. Ray introduced the school uniform of blue and brown. At the same time a school badge was designed with the motto "In fide scientia consistat" (Let knowledge be grounded in faith).
Photograph by Mrs. Nicole Partridge BA(Hons) of N. Spire Design Ltd.

By the late 1960s plans were already at an advanced stage for the building of Phase III at the "new" school. This final phase, costing £30,525.87, of which the managers' share was £4974, provided four junior classrooms, a library / TV bay, pottery studio, headmaster's room, storeroom, and a kitchen for the exclusive use of the parish. Some additional costs, and the valuation of the old school prior to its transfer to the parochial church council, had also to be taken into account. The architects were Matthew and Ashcroft, and the contractors J & R Fenton (Blackpool) Ltd.

The classrooms were brought into use in January 1970, and the school was dedicated and officially opened by the bishop Claxton of Blackburn on 4 June 1970. The total cost of all three building phases had been just over £53,200, and in his address bishop Claxton praised the work of the school managers who 'had raised more than £11,000 towards the cost of the school'.

He also thanked the Lancashire Education Authority, and through them the Department of Education and Science, who had provided the bulk of the rest of the cost. At the time of the official opening it was noted that the 'school has no endowments and the cost to the managers to build and to maintain the school has averaged £600 to £700 a year.'[89]

Bishop Claxton further noted that 'there was a very close and valuable

Opening of Phase III of the New Memorial School 1970
Rt. Rev. Charles Claxton (bishop of Blackburn), together with Eric Ray (headteacher) and Rev. Derek Sears (vicar of Freckleton 1966–74), at the official opening of Phase III of the New Memorial School on 4 June 1970. Bishop Claxton praised the school managers who he noted had 'raised more than £11,000 towards the cost of the school'.

Courtesy of George Eric Ray.

partnership between the Church and the county education authority in the building of schools', adding that 'partnership must be the operative word'. He concluded by saying that 'The partnership of parents was also needed', and that 'where there is a partnership of school and Church and home, then we believe that education will be a good education'.[90] With the opening of Phase III the "old" (Trinity) school closed, but it was not demolished until 1974.

In 1974, to mark the centenary of Freckleton as a separate ecclesiastical parish, a project, under the leadership of James Plummer, head of environmental studies, was undertaken by Class 2. Entitled "Freckleton Past and Present", it is an outstanding contribution to the history of the village and in the words of Mr. Plummer was intended to be a lasting "source of information".

At the conclusion of the project Mr. Plummer thanked all who had participated. In particular he thanked two pupils Karen Threlfall and Sheila Newton, who were described as the 'two girls who have been the spearhead of this project. In the latter stages of the project, they have contributed practically all the work involved'.

In 1976 a decision was made by the managers to use monies from the Platts Memorial Fund (which will be recalled was set up to assist 'needy grammar school children') to provide half the cost of providing the Bibles presented annually to school leavers. In 1988 monies in the fund were transferred to, and invested by, the Blackburn Diocesan Board of Finance.

In his report for 1977/78 Mr. Ray informed the governors that the year had commenced with 'a roll of two hundred and twenty one pupils and ended with two hundred and forty six'. Although this represented an increase of twenty five Mr. Ray noted that a 'downward trend has been noticeable for a few years and is likely to continue into the future'.

Mr. Ray added that along with the usual collections for charity, £47 had been raised during Lent for a project in Belize, and £468 for the Pat Seed Cancer Appeal. A group of junior pupils had also taken part in the May Day festivities on behalf of the Church Restoration Appeal. By the mid 1970s Mr. Ray had also arranged, every alternate year, a residential holiday during Whit

FRECKLETON PAST AND PRESENT PROJECT 1974
In 1974, to mark the centenary of Freckleton as a separate ecclesiastical parish, Class 2 undertook a project, under the leadership of James Plummer, entitled "Freckleton – Past and Present". Two pupils – Karen Threlfall (using click-wheel) and Sheila Newton – were described by Mr. Plummer as 'the spearhead of the project'.
School Archives.

School Staff – c1974
Back Row (L–R): James Plummer, Mrs. Williams, George Eric Ray (headteacher), Mrs. Stella Birkett, John Hull
Front Row (L–R): Mrs. Muriel Stirk, Mrs. Lilian Barker (school secretary), Miss Sheila Strother, Mrs. Jane Frame, Mrs. Margaret Salthouse (nee Kirby)
Courtesy of Mrs. Jane Frame, who also identified the members of the teaching staff.

week for volunteers from the ten to eleven age group. Places visited included York and Weston super Mare.

The late 1970s was a period of cuts in education budgets, and staffing levels were closely monitored. A letter from the Divisional Education Officer in February 1981 gave the teaching establishment at the school as 'headmaster +5' for the academic year 1981/2, meaning that the school would be overstaffed by one in September 1981. At the managers meeting in February 1981 Mr. Ray reported that, as he had predicted, there had been a slow decline in the number of pupils 'for a few years'. He added that one teacher would have to leave in 1981 'unless numbers increased'.

Changing social attitudes were reflected in a letter sent to the governors in June 1981 by Rev. Canon Beaumont, on behalf of the Blackburn Diocesan Council for Religious Education. In his letter he requested 'information about

Mrs. D. Graham and Miss Sheila Strother and Class of 1983
Back Row (L–R): John Woods, James Fellows, John Holloway
Fourth Row (L–R): Mrs. Graham, Rebecca Hesketh, Kate Nuttall, Dionne Whalley, Kathryn Fare, Michelle Camp, Diane Gates, Angela Cogan, Lynne Martin, Miss Strother
Third Row (L–R): Thomas Garlick, James Stead, Richard Imber, Stephen Harris, Leon Burgess, Andrew Stone, Andrew Woodruff
Second Row (L–R): Sarah Sanger, Helen Willis, Alison Gould, Sally Wade, Samantha Norton, Joanne Brookman, Lyn McGinty, Tracy Smith
Front Row (L–R): David Shergold, Not known
Courtesy of Mrs. Sue Wade, who also identified the pupils.

corporal punishment'. At the managers meeting in October 1981 the subject was discussed 'at length', and it was agreed that a clear statement on the policy would be put in the school brochure.

In February 1982 Mr. Ray informed the school managers that he had decided to seek early retirement, and four months later he formally submitted his resignation. In October the same year, although his request for early retirement had been refused, the managers, presumably in anticipation that retirement would soon be granted, appointed Mr. Gary H. Worthy to the provisional post of headteacher.

Mr. Ray presented his final report to the managers on 6 October 1982, in which he considered that he had a very stable staff who steered a middle course in the curriculum, and who worked consistently, and out of hours, with the P.T.F.A. arranging trips etc. He added that most schools leave activities outside school hours to parents only.

Mr. Ray further noted that the staff involved themselves in raising money for charity, and that £500 had recently been raised for the Fylde Hospice appeal; writing awards had been won by pupils; the cup at the local Horticultural Show had been won by the school for three consecutive years; the P.T.F.A. provided large sums of money for equipment etc, and there was no shortage of books or equipment; the school was used for evening classes by the Lancashire County Council, which was a good sign.

On 13 July 1983, his last day of service, Mr. Ray was presented with an Afghan Rug and an engraved goblet. Following the summer holiday school resumed on 1 September when seventeen new children were admitted to the

Netball Team 1987
Back Row (L–R): Lyn Martin, Dionne Whalley, Joanne Brookman, Lyn McGinty, Michelle Camp
Front Row (L–R): Helen Willis, Kathryn Fare, Tina Montgomery, Kate Nuttall, Diane Gates
Courtesy of Miss Helen Willis, who also identified the pupils.

reception class, and three to other classes making a total on the school roll of one hundred and fifty four. As Mr. Worthy was not able to take up his appointment until 1 January 1984 Miss Sheila Strother, the deputy head, became acting headteacher.

Gary H. Worthy commenced his duties as headteacher of Freckleton Church of England Primary School on 9 January 1984. His teacher training was at St Martin's Teacher Training College, Lancaster, and on qualifying as a teacher commenced his career at Cedar Street County Primary School, Blackburn. Prior to his appointment to Freckleton he was deputy head at St James Church of England School, Clitheroe.

He took over at Freckleton at a very crucial time in its development. Numbers on the roll had fallen to one hundred and forty children who were taught in just five classes. His remit was to build for the future, and raise the profile of the school within the Fylde region.

Mr. Worthy also had to contend with the numerous changes in education policy, and its resultant consequences. On 22 March 1984 he recorded in the log book that he had attended a headteachers meeting at Kirkham. The meeting was addressed by the divisional education officer who gave ' the annual gloomy picture in education – teacher's jobs to go, early retirement schemes, shortage of money'.

It was also a time of major changes in the way in which schools were to be governed, and in June 1984 the school managers were advised that a new governing body would have to be elected.

All this change notwithstanding, Mr. Worthy enthusiastically set about his task of taking the school forward. By the early 1980s it was obvious that computers would not only play an increasing role in teaching, but also become a tool within school administration. And on 19 May 1984 a barn dance at Garlick's Farm, organised by the P.T.F.A., raised £1000 for purchasing a computer for the school.

By February 1985 Mr. Worthy was able to report to the newly appointed school governors that the number on the school roll had increased to one hundred and seventy five, with twenty children down for admission in 1986, and a further twenty in 1987. In addition to core subjects more social and cultural activities were also taking place. On 15 February the whole school visited the Grand Theatre, Blackpool to see the musical "Charlie & the Chocolate Factory. And in May twenty five pupils and three staff, including Mr. Worthy, went on an 'Adventure Holiday' to the Isle of Man.

The first meeting of the new Governors was held on 6 March 1986. In the same year the Lenten Project raised £93.85 which was donated to the Church of England Children's Society. In 1987 the same project raised £125 for the N.S.P.C.C., and in 1988 £170 was raised for the Guide Dogs for the

Blind Association. In 1988 Mr. Worthy introduced "Book Week": a National Initiative which encouraged teachers to read a story to different classes for the last half hour of the school day.

The 1988 Education Act introduced the national curriculum, which included religious education as a nationwide curriculum for primary schools. It also introduced local management of schools (LMS) which allowed all schools to

Mrs. Margaret Salthouse (nee Kirby) and Class
150th Anniversary of Trinity School – 1989
To commemorate the 150th anniversary of the laying of the foundation stone for Trinity School the staff and pupils dressed in Victorian costume and studied the curriculum of the day.
Back Row (L–R): Liam Powney, Thomas Wade, Andrew Rawstrone, Thomas Bourne, Michael Rawcliffe
Third Row (L–R): Mrs. Salthouse, Leigh Cookson, Wesley Nuttall, John Rhodes, Andrew Calderbank, Mark Dolby, Liam Wyatt, Andrew Finch, Christopher Lowe
Second Row (L–R): Nicola Herne, Sarah Humphries, Suzanna Garlick, Kimberley Smith, Angela Wade, Amy Sanger, Laina Berry, Rachel Procter, Kerry Starr, Helen Stephenson
Front Row (L–R): Owen Hardman, Paul Dolby, Christopher Garlick, Andrew Cross, John Wilson, Graham Cogan
Courtesy of Mrs. Sue Wade, who also identified the pupils.

Re-dedication of the original (1839) Trinity School datestone
During the demolition of the "old" (Trinity) School Eric Ray recalled that George Rhodes (a school manager, and churchwarden of Holy Trinity 1959–1990) 'stood over the demolition team' who were 'very reluctant' to preserve either the datestone or foundation stone. The datestone was removed to the "new" school and placed in the school driveway. On 3 October 1989, as part of the 150th anniversary celebrations, the Rev. P. D. Hallett (right) (diocesan advisor) re-dedicated the stone at an open-air service. Rev. Hallett also presented the school with a commemorative plaque signed by the archbishop of Canterbury (president of the National Society). Next to Rev. Hallett is Rev. S. Brian (vicar of Freckleton 1988–1997).
Courtesy of Mrs. Jane Frame.

be taken out of the direct financial control of local authorities and handed to the head teacher and the governors of the school.

At the governors meeting held on 1 February 1989 Mr. Worthy reported on the many meetings he had attended regarding the new arrangements for LMS, and stressed that the role of a governor was now very important. He added that sub-committees would be needed to discuss various aspects and arrangements of management, and spoke of the details of the proposed national curriculum pointing out that eventually pupils would be tested at the ages of seven and eleven.

To mark the 150th anniversary of the school a "Victorian Day" was held on 3 October 1989 when the staff and children dressed in Victorian costume. At an open-air service the original Trinity School datestone was re-dedicated and placed near to the entrance of the present school. A commemorative plaque signed by the Archbishop of Canterbury, president of the National Society, was also presented to the school.

On 25 June 1992 the school hosted an "America Day": an event attended by seven veterans from the BAD2 association who had been stationed with the 8th United States Army Air Force at Warton during World War II. The work theme for class 6 was World War II, and there was also an "American Dinner".

Mrs. Jane Frame and Class of 1989
Back Row (L–R): Peter Hayhurst, Hannah Ikin, Katherine Schriber, Hayley Sinclair, Clair Croft, Hannah Baker, Mrs. Frame, Leanne Bonney, Adam Nelson, Paul Leckie, Andrew Monk, Craig Leckie, Zoe Cook
Middle Row (L–R): Jonathan Edwards, Kristy Wiggins, Bethany Plant, Jenna Schriber, Victoria Burton, Kate Denham, Ian Elsender, Lucy Earnshaw, Daniel Williams, John Moffat, Ryan Hardman, Andrew Leslie
Front Row (L–R): Daniel Thompson, Katie Errock, Natasha Coyne, Stephen Newton, Dean Simpson, Alyssa Mason, Kirsty Law
Courtesy of Mrs. Jane Frame. Pupils identified by Mrs. Kirsty White (nee Law), and John Moffat.

Mrs. Barbara McGuire and Gary Worthy (Headteacher) and Class of 1994–5
Back Row (L–R): Clare Rawstrone, Garry Livesey, Helen Warbrick, John Bourne, Angela Baker, Mark Dockray, Maxine Francis, Ashley Smith
Third Row (L–R): Mrs. McGuire, Karli Plant, Ryan Ashworth, Kay Scholz, Andrew Scholz, Tracey Hall, Jon Lee, Emma Threlfall, Daniel Procter, Heather Lowe, Mr. Worthy
Second Row (L–R): David Burton, Laura Lund, Lloyd Hardman, Kim Taylor, Christopher Staniford, Cara Hutchinson, Steven Wade, Samantha Wood
Front Row (L–R): Lucy Kay, Tommy Hoyles, Rachel Singleton, Vicky Swift, Richard Brook, Kimberley Frost, Matthew Ashworth, Jennifer Hodgson
Courtesy of Mrs. Ann Kay (nee Threlfall), who also identified the pupils.

Gary Worthy (headteacher) and Mrs. Barabara McGuire and Class of 1989
Back Row (L–R): Stephen Madden, David Parkinson, Mark Barnett
Third Row (L–R): Mr. Worthy, Howard Whiteside, Craig Connolly, Craig Law, Ryan Wear, Thomas Garlick, James Stead, Mrs. McGuire
Second Row (L–R): Angela Harbon, Caroline Edwards, Ann Shaw, Sally Wade, Gillian Whittle, Lynne Martin, Nicola Wilson
Front Row: Sarah Sanger

Courtesy of Mrs. Sue Wade, who also identified the pupils.

Leslie Turner
Leslie Turner was associate headteacher from January to September 2006, and substantive headteacher from September 2006 to August 2008.
Courtesy of Leslie Turner

Community events during the 1990s included the annual Lenten Project. In March 1993 the Spring Fair raised £680 which enabled new materials for infants, and geography and science text books for the juniors, to be purchased.

In the same decade the school football and netball teams were increasingly successful, and in 1993, at the Rural Fylde Swimming Gala held at Kirkham, the school won the large school league. In the same year 6 pupils spent several days at the Eden Valley Centre for Outdoor Pursuits. A memorial service was held at the school in August 1994 to commemorate the fiftieth anniversary of the 1944 air disaster.

In March 1996 Iain Martin, then head boy, took part in a national competition. He was chosen to record a synopsis of his dinosaur project at the school which was subsequently broadcast on BBC Radio 4. In June 1996 a charity concert was held in aid of the Bone Marrow unit at Manchester Children's Hospital. Pupils past and present, staff, and the school choir entertained and raised the sum of £240. And in October the same year, during Book Week, "Teddy Day" raised £710 in book sales, including £417 for class libraries.

The 1990s, however, is most notable as a decade of continuous change in education policy. In July 1991 statutory assessment tests (SATs) were introduced for seven year old pupils, and, in July 1995, for pupils aged eleven years. In 1992 a further Education Act resulted in school inspections no longer being carried out by H.M. Inspectors but by Ofsted (Office for Standards in Education).

When Ofsted inspectors visited the school in 1997 they hailed the quality of teaching as a strength of the school, and considered that 'in virtually every lesson it was satisfactory or better, and in many lessons it was very good and sometimes excellent'. The inspectors also noted that 'the school fostered positive values such as honesty and fairness' and that 'a very good range of extra-curricular activities were offered to pupils by dedicated staff'.[91]

In the same year there were two hundred and twenty four pupils on the roll, the highest total for twenty years. Mr. Worthy noted that parents were involved directly in school life, and offered valuable support to staff in a variety of ways. In 2001 the PTFA rebranded itself as "WISHES" (Working to Improve Standards of Happiness, Equality and Success), and whose ultimate aim was to 'have the support of every parent / carer to strengthen the links between Home and School for the benefit of every child'.

At the beginning of the present century the school had two hundred and twenty pupils, and under the requirements of the national curriculum the four core subjects were English, Maths, Science, and ICT. Foundation subjects were Music, Art, History, Geography, Religious Education, and Physical Education. Extra-curricular activities included various seasonal sports, a badminton club, and a choir.

In spring 2002 a school council was set up as part of the PSHE (Personal, Social, Health and Economic Education) programme, and representatives were elected by each class. And, in the same year, as part of the Queen's Golden Jubilee celebrations, each pupil was presented with a commemorative coin on the last day of term. Pupils also visited Winmarleigh Hall and Blackburn Rovers Education Centre (Year 6); Liverpool Museum (Year 5); Rufford Old Hall (Year 4); Deva Roman Experience in Chester (Year 3); Butterfly Farm in Williamson Park, Lancaster (Year 2); and Myerscough College Farm (Reception).

However, whilst, during the period 1997 to 2002, £100,000 had been spent on school building improvements, the considerable changes nationally, due to demographic changes in child population, were beginning to affect Freckleton. The governors had to initiate a programme of rationalisation due to loss of staff, including the post of deputy headteacher, and the merging of classes due to changes and major reductions in funding.

In his report of June 2003 Mr. Worthy observed that he considered 'the next twelve months is going to be very challenging for us as governors and for the teaching staff as they come to terms with the continued falling rolls situation'. He predicted that 'next September could see us down to one hundred and sixty five pupils'. However, somewhat ironically, there was money made available for school building improvements, and the school was successful in gaining finance for major work to the front of the school and the front offices. At the same time the stage area in the main hall was converted to become an IT suite.

Events in 2004 included a visit in June by astronaut David Scott, who had been a crew member of the Apollo 15 moon landing. And in August there was a memorial service to mark the sixtieth anniversary of the 1944

When the ICT Suite was created in the late 1990s utilising the former stage in the school hall it left a "white wall". In 2004 it was decided to cover the space with a permanent mural. A competition was held amongst the pupils to determine the design of the mural which was painted by three students at the University of Central Lancashire. The mural depicts school and church working together in the care of God's hands.

Photograph by Mrs. Nicole Partridge BA(Hons) of N. Spire Design Ltd.

air disaster. An American maple tree, the cost of which was funded by the Freckleton Memorial Trust, was planted in the school grounds in an area that subsequently became the Peace Garden.

In March 2005 Mr. Worthy advised the governors that

> You will, no doubt, have been informed of new changes in September this year regarding the re-modelling of the school workforce. This government initiative is building on reforms which came into force last September. The aims of these reforms are to raise standards for pupils and staff in schools, develop a career structure for support staff (they all have to undergo re-grading and re-determination of job descriptions) and to free teachers to teach, develop, plan and access

These changes also included a new system of short notice inspections carried out by Ofsted. Under this system headteachers were encouraged to complete a Self Evaluation Form (SEF) on a continual basis, which required them to be aware of strengths and areas for development. The SEF was considered crucial in evaluating the quality of leadership and management and the school's capacity to improve. Ofsted inspections were generally two day, or three day, visits every three years with two days notice.

During the period 2002 to 2005, due to legal changes there was an increase in parent governor representation to the governing body. Changes also occurred as to the roles and responsibilities for a governing body. Governors acquired more powers, but were also regularly open to election and re-election

Mr. Worthy retired as headteacher at Christmas 2005. He was replaced by Mr. Leslie Turner, initially as associate headteacher from January to September 2006, and as substantive headteacher from September 2006. Mr. Turner carried out his teacher training at Northern Counties College, Newcastle upon Tyne from 1967 to 1970. Prior to his appointment to Freckleton he held teaching posts at London, Gateshead, Southampton, and Morecambe.

In his report to the governors in March 2006 Mr. Turner observed that it was too early for him to have a firm and secure assessment of curriculum strengths, but noted that he had been impressed 'with the curriculum map in place, with the work done on "Assessment of Learning" and the learning ethos in the school'. He concluded by advising the governors that 'we must begin preparation for a new financial inspection procedure to be introduced' which he considered 'makes Ofsted look a little like a "teddy bear's picnic"'.

Opening of new classrooms – July 2011
In July 2011 the Rt. Rev. Nicholas Reade (bishop of Blackburn) visited the school to bless the new junior section buildings which had cost more than £330,000, and consisted of a learning centre as well as new classrooms. In this photograph the bishop is seen (L–R): with Alexandra Holloway (head girl), Mrs. Rachael Ainsworth (headteacher), Jessica Curtis (chairperson of school council).
School Archives.

Following an Ofsted inspection carried out on 21 and 22 November 2006 the school attained a Grade 2 (Good) in Achievement and standards; Personal development and well-being; Teaching and learning; Curriculum and other activities; Care, guidance and support; Leadership and management. The inspectors noted that 'this is a good and improving school. Pupils, parents and staff are delighted with the very good leadership of the headteacher, who already knows every child by name and has the gift of making each child feel special. The pupils tell us that he makes school fun'.[92]

The school building, however, was in need of further alterations and refurbishment. Consequently the governors and the school management team agreed to pursue an initiative to modernise the school environment over the following five to ten years.

It was a demanding challenge due to the fact that, as a voluntary aided Church School, the governors were required to directly fund ten per cent of any cost of any proposed building work in order to apply, and compete, for grants from the diocese, who in turn received funding from national government.

As has already been noted the original Trinity School was demolished in 1974. On 2 May 2007 the location of the school, and scene of the 1944 air disaster, was recorded by the unveiling of a plaque at the entry to Trinity Close. The event was described by the *West Lancashire Evening Gazette*

> This was the heartfelt message left by the people of Freckleton as they paid tribute to those who died in the village's air disaster of 1944.
>
> A large crowd gathered in the sunshine to watch a plaque being unveiled on the site of the old school where tragedy struck.
>
> Two children from Freckleton Church of England School were chosen to unveil the plaque.
>
> Mary Thompson, 11, who is the great-great-niece of disaster survivor Ruby Currell [nee Whittle], was chosen along with her classmate Thomas Lee, 10.

Mr. Turner resigned on 31 August 2008. Mrs. Sara Moreton, deputy headteacher, was appointed acting headteacher from September 2008 to August 2009. In September 2009, Mrs. Rachael Ainsworth took up her appointment as headteacher. Mrs Ainsworth's teacher training was at Charlotte Mason College, Ambleside. Prior to her appointment, at Freckleton, she worked in two other education authorities: Hertfordshire, teaching at Knutsford JMI School in North Watford; and Blackburn with Darwen, teaching at St. Paul's, Hoddlesden and St. Stephen's, Tockholes. On her appointment at Freckleton she inherited a school with one hundred and sixty four pupils.

In an extremely hectic first year Mrs. Ainsworth oversaw an Ofsted inspection within nine months of her appointment; a statutory inspection of Anglican schools (SIAS); a building project for three classrooms; and SATs testing. She had also put together a comprehensive school development plan which included the 'rigorous monitoring suggested by Ofsted'. A FAB Club (Breakfast Club & After School Club), originally proposed during the headship of Mr. Worthy, was also established.

In 2009, the governors, following a bequest from the Rhodes family which enabled them to fund their ten per cent of the total cost, were successful in competing for grant funding to carry out an extensive building programme. And from January to May 2010 work was carried out on alterations and refurbishment of the classrooms in the infant wing of the school. The alterations were subsequently blessed by the Rt. Rev. Geoff Pearson (suffragan bishop of Lancaster).

In the following year Mrs. Ainsworth was required to implement a plan for Finance Management Standards in School (FMSiS). This latter work was included in her report to the governors in September 2010, and it is an indication of her commitment to her new post that she concluded by adding 'not to mention many other moments of joy'.

Whilst an Ofsted inspection of 17 and 18 June 2010 noted that 'teaching overall is satisfactory',[93] the SIAS inspection, which also took place on 17 June 2010, took into account the 'disruption in school leadership which has now been addressed', and their inspector considered that

> The school is good in the way in which it meets the personal needs of all learners. The Christian ethos is very strong and is evident in all aspects of school life. The quality of care for all learners is very strong and the attention given to the pupils' personal development are both good.[94]

Further success in obtaining grant funding resulted in alterations of additional classrooms. And in July 2011, following a £330,000 refurbishment, a new junior section, consisting of a learning centre as well as new classrooms, was ready for use, and opened and blessed by bishop Reade of Blackburn.[95] In 2012, to mark the Diamond Jubilee of Queen Elizabeth II, the school was visited by Sir Richard Evans, a deputy lieutenant for Lancashire.

The most recent Ofsted report, carried out on 10–11 October 2012, resulted in the school being considered a "Good" school. In a summary of key findings for parents and pupils the inspectors considered 'this is a good school' because

> Pupils achieve well, making good progress from their individual starting points. Achievement is well above the national average by the time pupils leave school at the end of Year 6.

> There are clear procedures for the monitoring and development of teachers. These have contributed to improving teaching to good, resulting in higher standards in English and mathematics.
>
> Pupils enjoy school and this is reflected in their above average attendance.
>
> Pupils are very respectful of each other and their teachers.
>
> The school library is well-stocked with a wide range of reading material for pupils, supporting their love of reading.
>
> Pupils' behaviour is good making a strong contribution to their learning and to the school's positive ethos.
>
> Sharply focused and able leadership from the headteacher has ensured that the school has improved much since the previous inspection.
>
> Leaders, including the governing body, know the school's strengths and weaknesses. As a result they know what they have to do to improve further.
>
> Members of the governing body have a very good partnership with the headteacher and staff. They use this knowledge well to challenge and monitor the school's performance robustly.[96]

The school now (2014) offers on its site, Pre-school provision (2–4 years); Statutory education provision (4–11 years); Breakfast Club (4–11 years) – 7.30am–8.50am; After School Club (4–11 years) – 3.30pm–5.45pm. Thus as Freckleton Church of England Primary School, the successor to the original Trinity School, celebrates its 175th anniversary it is well placed to continue its important role in the life of the village into the foreseeable future.

Mrs. Rachael Ainsworth (Headteacher), Staff, and Pupils – Infants 2014

Photograph by Mrs. Nicole Partridge BA(Hons) of N. Spire Design Ltd.

Mrs. Rachael Ainsworth (Headteacher), Staff, and Pupils – Juniors 2014

Photograph by Mrs. Nicole Partridge BA(Hons) of N. Spire Design Ltd.

Freckleton Church of England Primary School – 2014

Photograph by Mrs. Nicole Partridge BA(Hons) of N. Spire Design Ltd.

APPENDIX A

Headmasters and Headteachers

(* Acting head)

John Worthington	1840–c1845
Thomas Walmsley	c1848–c1851
James Bryan	c1851–c1853
Thomas Cumberland	1857–1859
Wilfred Lees	1859–1861
Charles Everson	c1862–1864
John Heron	1864–1865
Robert Lupton	1865–1874
William Moorhouse Martin	1874–1882
John. N. Herbert *	1882 (Oct–Dec)
James Bramwell	1883–1914
Jane Elizabeth Hall *	1914 (May–Dec)
John Winchester	1914–1921
Edward Cross Rigby	1921–1923
John William Platts	1923–1939
Frederick Arthur Billington	1939–1968
George Eric Ray	1968–1983
Sheila Strother *	1983–1984
Gary H. Worthy	1984–2005
Leslie Turner	2006–2008
Sara Moreton *	2008–2009
Rachael S. Ainsworth	2009–

APPENDIX B

School Staff

(February 2014)

Headteacher	Mrs. R. S. Ainsworth
Deputy Headteacher	Mrs. J. Owen
Foundation Stage Teacher	Miss R. Woodrow
Year 1 Class Teacher	Mrs. L. Patterson
Year 2 Class Teachers	Mrs. V. Eaves & Ms. S. Prater
Year 3 Class Teachers	Mrs. R. Leaper & Mrs. S. Jenkins
Year 4 Class Teacher	Mrs. J. Owen
Year 5 Class Teachers	Mrs. F. Davies & Mrs. H. Reid
Year 6 Class Teacher	Mr A. Jones
Teaching Assistants	Mrs. J. Armitage, Mr. N. Bredbury, Mrs. L. Burwood, Mrs. S. Catterall, Mrs. R. Dey, Mrs. J. Hayward & Mrs. A. Jackson
School Secretary	Mrs. M. Ryland
Site Supervisor	Mr. I. Ferguson
Cleaner	Mrs. C. Thomas
School Cook	Mrs. P. Hogarth
Assistant School Cook	Mrs. J. Wilkinson
Welfare Assistants	Mrs. L. Bourn, Mrs. T. Clarke, Mrs. M. Fitzpatrick & Mrs. C. Ingledew

APPENDIX C

School Governors

(February 2014)

Chair of Governors, Foundation Governor	Mr. J. Martin
Vice-chair of Governors, Vicar of Freckleton	Rev. J. E. C. Percival
Headteacher, ex-officio	Mrs. R. S. Ainsworth
Associate Governor	Mrs. S. Dutton
Associate Governor	Coun. C. Robb
Foundation Governor	Ms. R. Bates
Foundation Governor	Mrs. G. Hughes
Foundation Governor	Ms. K. Press
Foundation Governor	Mr. J. Salthouse
Foundation Governor	Mr. A. Smith
Foundation Governor	Mr. R. Willets
Local Authority Governor	Mr. H. Robinson
Parent Governor	Mrs. N. Bell
Parent Governor	Mrs. A. Palmer
Staff Governor	Mrs. J. Owen

Notes

CC Christ Church, Oxford
LA Lancashire Archives (formerly Lancashire Record Office)
LPL Lambeth Palace Library
TNA The National Archives (formerly Public Record Office)

1 Cunliffe Shaw, R., *Kirkham in Amounderness* (R.Seed & Sons, Preston, 1949), p.466.
2 LA, WRW(A) 1724.
3 LA, FRP 13/1.
4 Freckleton Township disbursement book, 1803/4.
5 LA, QDV/9/21.
6 Freckleton Wesleyan Methodist Church Class Register, 1833–48.
7 LPL, ICBS 00905.
8 Preston Guardian 30 July 1904.
9 TNA, ED103/136/56.
10 Ibid.
11 Ibid.
12 Ibid.
13 CC, MS Estates 43 fol 949.
14 LA, DDCL 1186/27.
15 LA, PR 3216/11/1.
16 Preston Pilot 14 / 21 / 28 March 1840. This notice is also noteworthy as it refers to a previously unrecorded clergyman (Rev. J. R. Echlin M.A.) at Holy Trinity, Freckleton (see my History of Holy Trinity, Freckleton, published 2012). The Rev. Echlin was at Freckleton from 1838 until c1840, and would appear to have been resident in the village.
17 Preston Chronicle 20 June 1840.
18 Preston Pilot 30 May 1840
19 LA, DDCL 1195/25.
20 LA, DDCL 1199/3.
21 CC, MS Estates 43 fol 943.
22 Cunliffe Shaw, R., *The Records of a Lancashire Family* (The Guardian Press, Preston, 1940), p. 257.
23 TNA, ED103/79/26.
24 Preston Chronicle 13 August 1853.
25 Preston Chronicle 19 August 1854.
26 CC, MS Estates 43 fol 955.
27 Preston Chronicle 20 December 1856.
28 Preston Chronicle 27 December 1856.
29 Preston Chronicle 3 January 1857.
30 Preston Chronicle 9 October 1858.

31 Ibid.
32 CC, MS Estates 43 fol 993.
33 Preston Chronicle 13 April 1861.
34 LA, DP 376/1.
35 Shakeshaft, P., *The History of Freckleton* (Carnegie Publishing 2001), pages 188–190.
36 Preston Chronicle 10 October 1863
37 Preston Pilot 2 January 1864.
38 Lytham St Annes Express January 1941.
39 TNA, ED103/79/26.
40 TNA, ED 49/3714.
41 LA, Freckleton SP 120.
42 TNA, ED103//79/26.
43 Ibid.
44 Ibid.
45 Ibid.
46 LA, DP 376/4.
47 I am indebted to Mrs. Rachael Ainsworth the present headteacher, and former headteacher Mr. Gary Worthy, for allowing me free use of the school log books.
48 Preston Chronicle 21 December 1878.
49 TNA, ED 49/3714.
50 Ibid.
51 Newton Charity Minute Book.
52 Lytham, St Annes & Kirkham Sun 2 July 1887.
53 Ibid.
54 Ibid.
55 Recollections of the late Hannah Rayton (nee Brown).
56 Preston Chronicle 5 September 1891.
57 Newton Charity Minute Book
58 Information courtesy of George Mason, son of Richard Mason born 1900.
59 Recollections of the late Richard Rayton.
60 Recollections of the late Sylvester Till.
61 Information courtesy of Nellie Mason (nee Rigby).
62 Lancashire Daily Post 5 March 1925.
63 LA, PR 5010/3.
64 News Chronicle 24 August 1944.
65 Turner, Joyce., *The Freckleton Tragedy, 1944* (Landy Publishing, Staining , 2007).
66 TNA, ED21/54190.
67 Documents in possession of the author.
68 TNA, ED21/54190.
69 Lancashire Daily Post 6 September 1944.
70 Lancashire Daily Post 7 September 1944.
71 Ibid.
72 TNA, ED21/54190.
73 Lancashire Daily Post 19 September 1944.
74 Ibid.
75 Ibid.
76 TNA, ED21/54190.
77 Ibid.
78 Ibid.
79 Ibid.

80 Ibid.
81 Ibid.
82 Ibid.
83 Information courtesy of Gordon Porter.
84 Information courtesy of Stella Bowman (nee Bowling).
85 Information courtesy of Maureen Shakeshaft (nee Coates).
86 LA, CC / EM 18.
87 Lytham St Anne's Express 1 October 1954.
88 Information courtesy of Eric Ray.
89 Programme notes of Dedication and Official Opening.
90 Lytham St Anne's Express 11 June 1970.
91 Ofsted Report 8–11 December 1997.
92 Ofsted Report 21–22 November 2006. Inspection number 291456.
93 Ofsted Report 17–18 June 2010. Inspection number 339465.
94 SIAS Report 17 June 2010. SIAS number 430.
95 Lytham St Anne's Express 14 July 2011.
96 Ofsted Report 17–18 June 2012. Inspection number 401849.